Dear Bernard,

I have decided to give you this Book in Memory of Phil, and I hope as a very good friend over the years you will enjoy reading it.

Sincerely yours,

Pat Stephenson.

Sporting Rileys

Graham Robson

The Oxford Illustrated Press

ISBN 0 946609 21 7

Published by:
The Oxford Illustrated Press,
Sparkford, Near Yeovil, Somerset BA22 7JJ, England.

Haynes Publications Inc
861 Lawrence Drive, Newbury Park, California 91320 USA

British Library Cataloguing in Publication Data
Robson, Graham
  Riley sports cars 1926-1938.
  1. Riley automobile–History
  I. Title
  629.2'222   TL215.R5
  ISBN 0-946609-21-7

US Library of Congress
Riley Sports Cars:
86-81223

Printed in England by:
J.H. Haynes & Co. Ltd., Sparkford, Near Yeovil, Somerset BA22 7JJ.

Contents

Introduction and Acknowledgements

How could Riley produce a series of such splendid engines in the 1920s and 1930s, but sell so very few sports cars? How could Riley spend so much money on motor racing, yet fail so completely to capitalise on that success? Perhaps only Victor Riley and his family knew how — for even after completing the research for this book I can still offer no explanation — not even with the benefit of hindsight. A more modern analogy would be for Jaguar to have produced the XK twin-cam engine, won all those races with their C-Types and D-Types, yet not properly marketed the XK120s and E-types to back it up. Crazy — quite crazy.

Yet the sporting Rileys which were produced, seemingly reluctantly, and always in small numbers, were fine pieces of British engineering. Admittedly they were all (except for the Brooklands Nine) too heavy, and all somewhat under-powered and under-developed, but nevertheless nothing could hide their good looks, their fine engineering, and their great character. So why did so few people get to know about them, and why did so few people buy them instead of the more mundane machines that *did* sell in larger numbers? It made no sense then, and it makes no sense today.

This book, therefore, has been written to salute a series of beautiful, but rare, sporting cars, and to remind the latter-day motoring enthusiast of some splendid might-have-beens. Was not an MPH a more promising car than an SS100? Or an Imp more exciting than an MG Magnette? How did the Brooklands Nine compare with the Montlhery Midget? And how could the Riley magic fade so far into the 1950s, where the once-famous Blue Diamond graced nothing more interesting than the One-point-Five, Two-Point-Six and 4/68 models? How could a marque which had once been so important in the British motor industry be so defiled by the 'product planners' at BMC?

The Riley marque, once proudly advertised as being 'As Old as the Industry, As Modern as The Hour', was finally killed off by British Leyland in 1969, but the memory lingers on.

I am delighted to thank a large number of Riley enthusiasts who are quite determined to keep the cars alive, for helping me to produce this book:

I start with a special reference to Ian Hall, who not only owns the best-looking Sprite in the world, but took the trouble to give me advice and help at all stages, lent his cars for photography, and finally read through the manuscript to correct my mistakes. Ian and I first met in the Rootes rally team, but since then he has gravitated to Rileys, and I have moved on to four-wheel-drive rallying Supercars; there are times when I think he was better advised than me!

I also owe a lot to M.G. 'Griff' Griffiths, and to Tony Bird of the Riley Register, and to John Hall of the Riley Motor Club, for their help, and information. Barrie Gillies, Ian Gladstone, and Richard Odell all talked to me, at length about sporting Rileys (and how to rebuild them), and it was Mark Gillies, Barrie's son, who kindly agreed that my chapter on racing Rileys was not going to cut across his plans for producing a complete treatise about the amazingly successful Riley competitions programme of the inter-war years period.

Mirco Decet took most of the pictures, and joins with me in thanking Dr. Roger Andrews, Tim Dyke, the Rev. Canon John Gathercole, Henry Geary, Colin Ryder and Richard Wills for rolling out their fine sporting Rileys to be photographed.

Michael Ware of the National Motor Museum, and Michael Barker of the Midland Motor Museum both provided invaluable assistance as did, in their own ways, Chris Harvey, and my SS100-owning chum, John Parker.

Finally, where would any historian be without the ability to quote from the most authoritative motoring magazines? Throughout this book there are references, and direct quotations, from Riley features first seen in *The Autocar, Motor, Motor Sport,* and *Road and Track,* which I am happy to acknowledge. Without them — and particularly without *Motor Sport* — the Riley reputation might have died away completely.

Finally, the publication of this book celebrates an important date. 1986 is the sixtieth anniversary of the launch of the twin-high-cam Riley Nine engine. Does the timing of a book on sporting Rileys need a better excuse than that?

Graham Robson,
Burton Bradstock,
Dorset, January 1986

Colour Plates

Plate 1 The four-door Redwinger with its all-weather protection.

Plate 2 A Brooklands Nine ex-factory race car, registered KV 5392, showing the cycle-type wings and aero-screen.

Plate 3 A Brooklands Nine had just enough room for two passengers.

Plate 4 The race-prepared 1,087-cc engine of Richard Wills's ex-works Brooklands Nine.

Plate 5 The familiar radiator, free-standing headlamps, and front end of one of the rare March Specials.

Plate 6 Colin Ryder's March Special.

Plate 7 Is a Lynx a sporting Riley or not? I think so.

Plate 8 Some Lynxes had two doors, and some four, but all had close-coupled four-seater accommodation.

Plate 9 The Ulster Imp was a rare racing derivative of the Imp, first built in 1934.

Plate 10 The Imp of 1934 was a smart little car, closely related in many ways to the larger-engined MPH.

Plate 11 Rear view of John Gathercole's Imp.

Plate 12 BLN 39, is a well-known MPH, and shows off the thoroughbred lines to perfection.

Plate 13 The side-view of an MPH is much like that of the Imp, and so it should be; they share some panels and chassis engineering.

Plate 14 Ian Hall's beautiful black Sprite, with that characteristic 'waterfall' grille shared with no other Riley sports car.

Plate 15 The Sprite rear style, though clearly derived from that of the MPH, featured more flowing rear wings.

Plate 16 The facia of the Sprite.

Plate 17 The Riley Sprite appeared at about the same time as did BMW's 328, and both had the same ideas of a modern nose style.

Plate 18 A 1924 four-seater Redwinger.

Plate 19 A 1936 Riley special at Cadwell Park.

Plate 20 Hector Dobb's offset single-seater racing Riley.

Plate 21 A. N. Farquhar's racing Brooklands Seven, at Cadwell Park in 1985.

Plate 22 AKV 218 was the original prototype Sprite but is now much modified.

Plate 23 Richard Odell's racing Redwinger in action.

Plate 24 The engine of the racing Redwinger.

Plate 25 Ian Hall's splendidly presented Sprite engine.

Plate 26 Sprite in action.

I
Riley: The Family Company 1896 – 1938

Is there still anyone out there who does not know the essential difference between a *real* Riley and a 'Nuffield' Riley? I hope not. However, right at the beginning of this book, I want to make it quite clear that I only intend to cover the sporting cars, and engines, which were developed and built while the Riley family controlled the business — which means that my story effectively ends just before the outbreak of the Second World War.

A few definitions, therefore, will be helpful before I go any further into the technical stories. Until 1938 the various Riley businesses were controlled, and operated by members of the Riley family, and all two, three and four-wheeled machines carrying that name were assembled in Coventry. Thereafter the scene — and the parentage of the various cars carrying Riley badges — became confused. At first 'Nuffield' Rileys were assembled in the old Riley factories in Coventry, then this job was moved to another Nuffield factory, the MG factory at Abingdon. The final generation — of what I choose to call 'BMC Rileys' — were assembled either at Abingdon, Cowley (ex-Morris) or Longbridge (ex-Austin)!

The overlap, too, between 'Coventry' Rileys and 'Nuffield' Rileys, was considerable, for the very first post-Second World War Rileys (the RM models) were designed by Riley-Coventry, while the famous twin high-camshaft Riley engines ($1^{1}/_{2}$-litre and $2^{1}/_{2}$ litre four-cylinder units) were not only used in 'BMC' Rileys until 1957, but found their way into the Healey sports cars built until the early 1950s.

It is important that we understand the roots, and the origins, of the company. These lay, in the first place, with William Riley, whose family were originally weavers, and it all began in the city of Coventry.

Before the onset of the Industrial Revolution, Coventry was tiny, but by the mid nineteenth century its population had rocketed, industrial times had changed, and the two principal industries were watch-making, and ribbon-weaving. The Riley family became Master Weavers, and not only produced material, but also manufactured weaving machinery. William Riley came to manage this business from 1870.

By this time, however, Coventry was experiencing industrial upheaval.

Strikes at home, and competition from overseas, hit hard at the weaving industry. Before long, factories were closing down, and unemployment was rising fast.

One result of this was that entrepreneurs looked around for alternative projects. The most successful of these was the new sewing machine industry. James Starley was one of the founding members, who went on to build pedal cycles. Within twenty years several ambitious young men left his employ to start their own businesses. Some of the motor industry's most famous marques — Rover and Hillman among them — developed in this way.

Riley, for their part, stayed aloof from such fashions for many years, but by 1890 the family needed to diversify so that they could stay in business. In that year, therefore, William Riley bought up the Bonnick cycle-making business, which was producing two-wheelers at King Street, in Coventry.

This enterprise flourished, in spite of vigorous competition from all the other competitors in the city, and on 23 May 1896 the Riley Cycle Co. Ltd came into existence. It was from that base that the Riley motor car manufacturing business eventually developed.

At this time there seemed to be Riley personalities everywhere in the organisation. William, Basil, and Herbert Riley were all involved in that original cycle-producing business in 1896, while William's sons — Allan, Cecil, Percy, Stanley and Victor — were all vigorous young men, rapidly becoming entranced by the prospects for that new-fangled invention, the motor car.

[At this point I ought to recall that the country's very first motoring magazine, *The Autocar,* had been started up, in Coventry, in 1895, and that the first Coventry-built cars — Daimlers, licence-built from the German Daimler concern — were just going on sale. The era of Coventry, as a 'motor-city', was just beginning.]

The first ever Riley motor car, a one-off prototype, was designed and built by Percy Riley between 1896 and 1898, but was never put into production, and for the next few years the company concentrated on applying its knowledge of internal combustion engine power to bicycles, tricycles, and even to quadricycles. The very first engine-powered Riley four-wheeler (the Royal Riley Quadricycle) was shown at the National Cycle Show at Crystal Palace in 1899.

In the meantime, Riley had set up a new subsidiary company (the Riley Engine Company), to design and build its own power units, to take over from the proprietary engines which had been used at first. The directors of the new enterprise were Percy, Victor and Allan Riley, and it was Percy who began to make his name as the top designer in the concern.

By 1904 the Cycle Co. was concentrating on the production of engine-powered Tricars, which were distinguished by the fitment of a passenger's seat ahead of the handlebars (and ahead of the driver!) — which

must have been a very exciting position to take, if not actually a perilous one, when the machine was threading its way through heavy traffic.

At first, of course, the Tricars were really nothing more than modified motorcycles, but after a couple of years they were beginning to look altogether more sophisticated, with steering wheels instead of handlebars, and with more complete bodywork and weather protection. The scene was now set for the production of the first true four-wheeler Riley motor car.

If we forget the prototype Quadricycle of 1899 (and I now propose to do so . . .), then the first Riley car was built in 1905, and went on sale in 1906. It was not at all an exciting, or technically advanced design, though it seems to have been surprisingly sporting. The engine was a water-cooled 60-degree vee-twin unit of 1,034 cc, had its crankshaft transversely mounted, and drive through a gearbox alongside it in the frame, with final drive to the rear axle being by chain.

The engine/transmission assembly, by the way, was under the seats, rather than ahead of the driver. Front and rear suspension was by cantilever quarter-elliptic leaf springs, the chassis frame was tubular, and the complete two-seater cost £168 (160 guineas). Called the '9 hp' model, it actually had an engine which could develop up to 12 bhp if pressed.

Percy Riley had designed both the engine and the transmission, thus establishing a precedent which persisted until the 1930s, and gave the marque much continuity and 'pedigree'. Other companies hired designers to produce their cars, but Riley found sufficient expertise among the members of its own large family!

So typical of the 'vintage' scene in Britain, and at Riley — this was a 1920s-style side-valve model on the Connel Bridge, in Scotland. The four-seater Redwinger was developed from this type of car.

There was still a long way to go before the first of the true Sporting Rileys came on to the scene, for the first of the advanced twin-high-camshaft engines would not be launched until 1926. The original 9 hp model, in fact, had a considerably more advanced layout than any of the cars which succeeded it. In the next twenty years Rileys progressively fell more and more into line with the accepted type of specification which featured in so many British cars.

Before there were Brooklands Nines, there were ordinary Nines — this being a four-seater tourer on the Land's End trial.

The second range of Riley cars, the 12-18 hp model, had its engine at the front of the car, with a propeller shaft driving the rear wheels, along with a parallel torque member to provide accurate rear suspension geometry.

It was not until 1913 that the first four-cylinder Riley motor car, the 17-30 hp model, was put on sale. This was even more conventional than earlier models, for it had an in-line, side-valve, water-cooled engine of 2,951 cc, torque tube propeller shaft drive to the back axles, and half-elliptic leaf spring suspension at front and rear. In the meantime, there had been corporate changes in the business, with these cars eventually being produced by Riley (Coventry) Ltd.

In 1919, after there had been an enforced four-year lay-off due to the First World War, Riley produced a new range of cars. These were the 11 hp models; the first Rileys to carry the famous vee-style radiator, which

The car that started the Little Redwinger story: the standard-bodied two-seater which Victor Wallsgrove took on the Scottish Six Days Trial in 1922 . . .

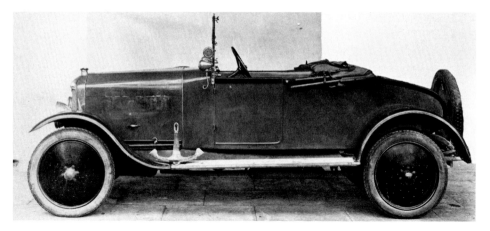

proudly carried the Riley diamond-shape badge. Even so, although it was a 'post war' car, its engineering was still far removed from that which was to follow later in the decade. Nevertheless, it was the first chassis on which a genuine sporting Riley version was produced.

The layout, however, was utterly conventional, for the chassis had minimal cross-bracing, open propeller shaft drive to the back axle, half-elliptic springs, no dampers and no front brakes. The engine was an uninspired four-cylinder side-valve.

At this time, however, the memorable advertising slogan 'As Old as the Industry' was adopted, and the first sporting two-seaters (not then called the Redwingers) came along in 1921. In the next few years the engine was slightly enlarged, and made more powerful, while alternative body styles were also made available.

All this, as we now see, was merely a prelude to the 1926 Olympia Motor Show, and to the launch of an all-new Riley — the legendary 9 hp model. Then, as later, Riley had a rather sprawling business, not only with several factories dotted around Coventry, but with a complex financial structure. It was a mini-empire which produced rather more of its motor cars (including engines, transmissions, and a wide choice of body shells) than some of its rivals. This fact, plus the numbers of cars produced in a year being fairly small, must have made it difficult to compete on price with other firms, who tended to buy-in their hardware from other companies. Not that Riley minded this in later years, as they could, and often did, boast about the throroughbred character of their machines.

The new 9 hp range went on sale at the beginning of 1927, and the last of the old side-valve cars was built in 1928, after which every 'Coventry' Riley car would be fitted with one or other of the twin high-camshaft engines which were produced in the next decade or so.

All these engines were four-cylinder units at first, but the first straight 'six' (a development of the 'four' — the 14-6) came along in 1928. Almost as soon as the 9 hp 'Brooklands' model went on sale, Riley's motor racing activities also began to gather momentum, and there would be many successes (and some heartbreaking failures) to recall in the 1930s.

Rather surprisingly, Riley survived the serious British slump of the early 1930s (companies like Bentley and Lanchester went under), and by the mid-1930s they had bounced back so much that they were producing a large range of cars, and no fewer than four different engine layouts: the four-cylinder 9 hp, the six-cylinder, the vee-eight cylinder, and the latest 1½-litre 'four'.

Yet another new engine, the 2½-litre 'Big Four', came along in 1937, by which time Riley had also become involved in another motoring venture, the Autovia car, which used *another* vee-eight engine with different castings, and a considerably larger cylinder capacity. All this frenzied diversity, with too many models being built in too limited quantities, must have hit the company's finances very hard indeed, especially when the expense of motor racing was added in. Unfortunately, the company's annual reports do not seem to have survived. We do know however, that in the year ending 31 January 1936 a handsome profit of £68,897 was made, but that it was reported the next set of figures, due in the summer of 1937 would be ominously late and that when they were revealed, there would be a substantial loss to declare. To dedicated Riley enthusiasts this was a real shock, for before this time there had apparently been year after year of calm profit making.

With sales flagging, and the demand for sporting Rileys dried up, the financial roof fell in, in February 1938. It was at that point that Victor

. . . and this is the starkly-equipped aluminium body style which it was given later in the year. Wallsgrove himself is at the wheel.

Riley, who was chairman and managing director of the company, stated that:

> 'The directors have given long and anxious consideration to the financial position of the company, and in view of the difficulties experienced in carrying on the business, they have felt constrained to ask the Company's bankers to appoint a receiver to protect the assets in the interests of all concerned.'

It also became clear that Riley had been negotiating with the Triumph concern, also of Coventry, with a view to merging, but this would have been a real 'frying pan into the fire' move, as Triumph was also in financial difficulty, and also anxiously looking over its shoulder to see the creditors closing in!

The only practical way out (though it hurt a lot of people, and their careers), was to close down loss-making activities, and sack a lot of staff. Autovia was sold off, the racing programme was cancelled, and several slow-selling models were discreetly dropped.

With Sir W. H. Peat as the receiver, the much-chastened company staggered on for several months, in 1938. What happened next is summarised in *The Life of Lord Nuffield,* (by P.W.S. Andrews and Elizabeth Brunner, now long out of print):

> 'It is also said that its [Riley] management fell apart after the death of its founder, when the business passed to his five sons ... Whatever the precise reason for its position in 1938, Riley's was in danger of being wound up. Mr. Victor Riley therefore appealed to Nuffield to save it by taking it over, and he decided to do so. He [personally] bought the business for some £143,000 and . . . resold Riley's almost at once to Morris Motors, for the nominal sum of £100 . . . When it became a subsidiary of Morris Motors, Mr. Victor Riley took charge of his old firm as managing director . . .'

So ended the independence of one of Coventry's most distinguished motor car manufacturers. The Riley line of cars lived on until 1955, with the Coventry-designed RM series models being built at Coventry, and from 1949 at Abingdon, while the last twin-high-camshaft unit was fitted to the Riley Pathfinder saloons, which were also assembled at Abingdon.

Even so, in the 1926 to 1938 period, it had been an exciting, and exhilarating, ride, for all lovers of fine Riley cars. From time to time there had been financial and commercial problems, but some fine sporting cars had been produced along the way. The puzzle, then as now, is to understand why they did not sell in larger quantities.

Now, therefore, it is time to analyse the careers of the real thoroughbred Rileys of that period.

II

Sporting Rileys: The Four-Cylinder Models (including the side-valve cars)

This chapter has to deal with several different Riley models, and with two entirely different types of car. The first Sporting Rileys surveyed are the side-valve cars, eventually (but not initially), known as Redwingers, while all the other four-cylinder cars described had one of the several different types of twin high-camshaft engines, which were remarkably advanced for the period, and which had part-spherical combustion chambers, and cross-flow breathing.

At first glance, nothing could be apparently less sporting than the Riley Eleven h.p. family of new cars which was announced in the autumn of 1919, though it was from this unpromising beginning that the well-known Redwinger sporting model was developed. In the beginning, the first Elevens had a simple chassis, with a 9-foot wheelbase, parallel-sided, channel-section side members, beam axles front and rear, no damping of any sort, and no front wheel brakes. There were bolt-on disc wheels at first, even though Riley had developed bolt-on wire spoke wheels for their pre-war models.

The engine was a rugged, no-nonsense, side-valve four-cylinder unit (bore and stroke 65.8 x 110 mm, 1,498 cc), with an aluminium crankcase, a separate cast iron cylinder block, and a three-bearing crankshaft splash lubricated with troughs, replenished by a low-pressure pump, for the big ends to dip in. In standard form this engine developed 35 bhp at 3,200 rpm.

There was a cone clutch, but the gearbox was separated from the clutch by a short Cardan shaft, and there was a sizeable vintage-style radiator (the first in the now-classic Riley between-wars style), so arranged as to encourage thermosyphon cooling. You could have looked, and looked hard, but found no trace of a sporting pedigree to come.

There were, on the other hand, several advanced features by 1919 standards, which included aluminium pistons, a four-speed gearbox, self-lubricating bushes in the chassis, and only six greasing points which had to be lubricated at six-monthly intervals.

Only two different Riley (Midland Motor Body Company, actually — a subsidiary company) bodies were shown at first, but within months there

This four-seater Redwinger (also pictured in the colour section), is an original Riley works demonstrator, in absolutely typical trim for the period.

was a choice between four shells — one a two-seater selling for £520, the other a smart Coupé for £600. Apart from the Riley radiator, and the wheel disc covers, the styling was much like that of any other post-Armistice car,

The smoothly-styled front wings of the Redwinger, surrounding the bolt-on wire-spoke wheels.

Four-seater Redwingers had this distinctive four-pane windscreen so arranged as to allow ventilation, but no direct draught, into the car.

and with prices at such relatively high levels the rate of production was always likely to be low.

Riley's problem, one shared with most other British companies of the day, was that all costs were rising rapidly immediately after the war, at the same time as the brief sales boom was collapsing. For 1921, Riley hoped a customer would pay £630 for a two-seater Eleven, and up to £850 for a saloon version. The market-leader was Morris, whose 'Bullnose' prices started at £465, but these would be cut, quite considerably, in the next twelve months. To follow Morris down, in an attempt to remain competitive, Riley price cuts were also inevitable, so at the 1921 Olympia Show the price of the Two Seater 'Sports' was cut back to £520. The 'Sports', incidentally, gained that name only because of its rather rakish styling, rather than from a special chassis, or from any established record of success in motor sport. Only in name was it the predecessor of the Redwingers which were to follow.

At this point the very significant personality of Victor Wallsgrove comes into the story, for it was he, not Victor Riley, or Harry Rush (who had designed the side-valve car) who was really responsible for turning the 'Eleven' into a proper sports car.

Wallsgrove was born in Warwick, worked in the motor industry as a young man, moving from firm to firm (perhaps as a result of his apparently brash, opinionated personality), then served throughout the First World War, before joining Riley, to become assistant works manager.

Once installed, he began competing in trials (the predecessor of

Four-seater Redwingers, much the most numerous type, had a huge amount of rear-seat space. In some ways modern cars are not as useful as the older variety.

Above right: The rear quarter of the Redwinger naturally featured re-painted wings, and there was good weather protection by the standards of the period.

The simple instrument layout of the Redwinger included a large clock ahead of the passenger, and the speedometer ahead of the driver. The handbrake is in the centre of the floor, the gear lever closer to the steering wheel.

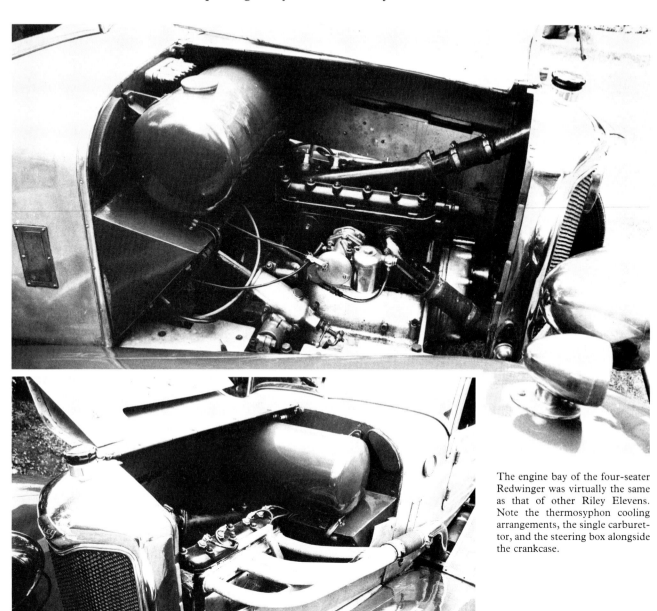

The engine bay of the four-seater Redwinger was virtually the same as that of other Riley Elevens. Note the thermosyphon cooling arrangements, the single carburettor, and the steering box alongside the crankcase.

The left-side of the Redwinger engine bay shows the free-flow exhaust system on this ex-works demonstrator, now owned by Dr. Andrews.

long-distance rallies) using standard-bodied Rileys. In mid-1922 he took over a 'works' two-seater Eleven (registered HI 104 — which is an Irish registration, and no-one now seems to know how this came to be in the factory at the time), and entered it for the Scottish Six Days Trial.

The simple Redwinger front suspension and steering layout, featuring Hartford friction dampers, but no front brakes.

In a good fairy-tale, I would be able to report a sensational victory . . . but in fact the Wallsgrove Riley was eliminated in the closing stages with magneto failure. Before then, however, his had been the oustanding performance of the trial, with outright fastest performances set on several speed tests, against competition which included cars as formidable as Brescia Bugattis.

Clearly this gave him a great deal of encouragement — if a standard car with a standard body could achieve so much, what might be done with a lightweight machine? Later in the summer, therefore, he took the body shell off the trials car's chassis, and had a stark new two-seater aluminium body shell fitted instead. No doubt it was Wallsgrove's own wish that the body panels should be polished, but otherwise unpainted, and that the wings, chassis and new wire spoke wheels should all be painted bright red. This was really the beginning of the Redwinger story. That very first car had no doors, and a long pointed tail, with the spare wheel carried on the side of the scuttle, ahead of the driving compartment.

Not only did Riley make Wallsgrove their official competitions manager at this time but they decided to promote the sporting image that Wallsgrove had inspired. For 1923 (first deliveries were made early in that year), the aluminium-bodied two-seater was put on sale, and this was soon joined (by the end of 1923) by an aluminium-bodied four-seater, which looked very much like the existing 'All Seasons' model. Priced at £495, they had guaranteed top speeds of 70 mph (two-seater) and 60 mph (four-seater).

At this stage, however, they were still not Redwingers, and the first batch did not have red wings anyway! At first they were fitted with unpainted aluminium wings, but these were soon seen to suffer damage from flying stones, so a change was made to steel wings, and the red painting also became normal. However, as Redwinger expert Richard Odell told me, one must never be dogmatic about Riley specifications, for in later years some cars did not have red wings: from the start of the 1926 model year some had the aluminium coachwork painted, and a few may

Richard Odell blasting over Southport sands in 1982 in his short-chassis Redwinger 'sand-racer', repeating exploits first set up nearly 60 years earlier. Note the 'clam shell' wings, and the door-less two-seater style.

Richard Odell races his 8 foot wheelbase Redwinger 'sand-racer' in the 1980s, no less vigorously than it was campaigned in the 1920s. The pump near his right hand is to supply fuel pressure. In spite of the 'single-seater' looks, and character, this car uses many near-standard Riley Redwinger chassis components.

even have had the larger engine (introduced for the Twelve at the Olympia motor show in 1924)!

From 1922 until 1928 (though very few were built after the introduction of the Nine in 1926/7) there were aluminium-bodied Riley sports cars on sale, and although the mainstream Riley became a Twelve for 1925, with a much more robust chassis, the sports cars normally retained the slimmer original frame. There was, of course, little point in any owner opting for the larger engine if he had any intention to compete in motor sport, for the Twelve's capacity was 1,645 cc, which put it above the 1,500 cc class limit.

Rileys themselves built the bodies, and although the two-seater bore a certain resemblance to the 'ducks-back' Alvis 12/50, and also to the Triumph 10/20 of the period, it seems certain that each of these three Coventry concerns 'did its own thing', all producing styles which were *à la mode* for 1923.

We know little about the performance of the Redwingers, except by hearsay, though *The Autocar* tested a 'non-Redwinger-type' £450 four-seater Sports model for nearly 1,000 miles at Whitsuntide in 1923 (this drive is described in more detail in Chapter IV), and made little of the performance, stating no figures, but did note that 'the car ran beautifully', and reported an overall fuel consumption (which included taking part in the Edinburgh Trial), of 32 mpg.

For 1925 there was a revised range of side-valve Rileys, but it was the Olympia Show at which the original-type Redwingers were finally named. The name, for sure, had not officially appeared in catalogues before this time, but by 1926 the enthusiastic owners of early cars who wrote to magazines like *The Autocar* were calling their 1924 models by that name in any case!

The booklet published by Riley at the time insisted that the cars were still officially known as 'Two-seater Sports' and 'Four-Seater Sports', but in the two-seater section the company admitted that

'. . . those who are in any way familiar with Riley cars call it the "Little Red Winger". Indeed it is the pet of the Riley range and if real affection has ever been lavished on any car at all, then the Riley sports has had its quota.

'70 mph is guaranteed in all cases, and on the track as much as 90 miles per hour has been attained . . .'

'Beautifully designed, the effect of the shining aluminium body, toning with the cardinal red of the wings, chassis, wheels and upholstery is remarkable . . . The seats, upholstered in red hand-buffed leather, are slightly staggered to give the driver perfect freedom for quick and easy change. There are two independent windscreens, Triplex glazed, of special and pleasing design, and hood and all-season equipment are fitted . . .'

Some Brooklands Nines were even fiercer than others! This beautiful ex-works car, generally acknowledged as the 'most raced' of all Brooklands, is owned by Richard Wills, as is the much larger, and heavier, Lagonda behind it.

The racing Brooklands Nine, like the road-car from which it was derived, used a low-slung chassis, and had a skimpy two-seater style. The rare road cars had differently-shaped wings.

The tail of the Brooklands was mostly full of fuel tank, but although this is an ex-works racer, it is in full road trim.

The booklet had no less to say about the four-seater, which was a four-door model with more comprehensive weather protection. It weighed considerably more, and had different gearing and a larger screen (and, therefore, drag), which explains why the guaranteed top speed was only 60 mph, although it still sold for the same price — £495.

The two-seater was a stark machine, which sold only in limited numbers compared with the four-seater, and although I might be wrong to describe the all-weather protection as a joke, it was certainly barely adequate. If an owner took delivery with the twin aero-screens, no hood could really keep out the weather. If he ordered the car with the full-width but nevertheless cut-down glass screen his prospects were better; in both cases the hood hung over the top of this screen, and was secured to the scuttle by what might be described as 'pram straps'. There were no side curtains.

The chassis followed the general lines of the touring models, and the same 4 foot 4-inch wheel tracks were retained. By this time front brakes were available as optional extras, and Hartford friction dampers were fitted. Mechanically the Redwinger was still not at all advanced, for its engine had only three crankshaft bearings, and there were no balance weights on that shaft, though the power output had been increased, to 40 bhp at 3,600 rpm. The engine, in fact, could be persuaded to turn over at 4,000 rpm, which was no mean speed for the period. The cone clutch was distinctly 'Edwardian' in its outlook, gears were engaged by sliding the pinions into mesh, and the long gearlever stuck straight up from the top of the gearbox itself. A few cars, according to Arnold Farrar, were built with right-hand gear change.

The attraction of the Redwinger, however, lay in its body style, and

Above left: Brooklands chassis in detail, showing the front suspension, the Hartford dampers, and the wing and headlamp support arrangements.

Above: At the time, most Brooklands Nine owners thought the brakes were inadequate. Maybe – but Riley made every attempt to keep them cool and well-ventilated

Richard Wills's ex-works Brooklands Nine has big rear brakes, with well-ventilated drums. It competed at Le Mans, winning the Rudge Whitworth Bienniel Cup in 1934, averaging 68.33 mph for 24 hours.

the character it exuded. In some ways this was due to the use of a standard 'early 1920s Coventry' style, whether two-seater or four-seater, which was all about function, and included no superfluous decoration. The body shell was as slim as the chassis frame itself, which meant that space across the shoulders, especially in the two-seater, was at a premium.

Two spare wheels were often carried, mounted one each side of the scuttle, and the line of the wings themselves was quite distinctive. Front wings swept straight back to the base of the running board under the door itself, while the rear wings of the two-seater swept gracefully up from that short board at an angle, rather than straight up like most conventional cars.

Two other Redwinger derivatives should now be mentioned — one because a pristine example survives, and is raced, to this day, the other because it seems never to have proceeded beyond exhibition at the Olympia motor show!

Riley's star of the 1924 Olympia Motor Show was what their booklet called the 'Short Wheelbase Sports', which was offered: '. . . to meet the demands of those motorists who desire to attain even higher speed than that attainable on the other models illustrated.'

Once again, this had originally been a bright idea by Victor Wallsgrove, who had chopped the wheelbase of an original frame to a mere 8 feet and drilled large holes in the chassis to 'add lightness'. Naturally there were no doors fitted to the skimpier body which had oyster-shell front and rear wings, and an even shorter tail; Wallsgrove used it to go sand-racing at Southport, Skegness, Weston-super-Mare, and similar locations.

This splendid car, registered RW 104, and owned by Richard Odell for the past decade, is still raced today, and it was a replica which was put on sale at the end of 1924. The price at first was 'on application', but set at £545 by 1925. The fact is, however, that there was almost no demand for such a car, for Odell maintains that only three were ever made in 1925 before the car was dropped after one season.

The original 'sand-racer' was certainly super-tuned to go racing, but the car offered at Olympia had the same running gear as any other Redwinger. With the 40 bhp engine, it is likely that the top speed was about 80 mph, though Richard Odell's 'works' machine is considerably quicker than this, and can deal with $4^1/2$-litre Bentleys in modern VSCC racing!

The 11/50/65 Supercharged Sports model was shown at Olympia in 1926, when most Riley attention was being paid to the all-new Nines. It was a four-seater with the characteristic aluminium body and red wing colour schemes, but the engine was very different from standard. Not only was there a Roots-type supercharger, driven from the nose of the crankshaft, but the engine had been converted to overhead valves!

The supercharger installation was quite conventional (it was fitted neatly under a cut-out in the radiator), for it sucked fuel/air mixture in from a single carburettor mounted above and behind it on the left side of the engine, before blowing it into the engine. The controversy, however, was caused by the overhead valve conversion of the 1,498 cc engine, which was immediately seen to be a copy of another design — almost certainly that of the Alvis 12/50 (which had evolved from an earlier, side-valve, 12/40 unit in 1923). Apparently, after the question of patent infringement had been raised, Rileys dropped the project, which was never again seen in public, and certainly never put on sale.

The 'Little Redwingers' had a small, but devoted, following in the mid 1920s, at a time when very few sports cars were in any case being sold. As soon as the Nine went on sale the Redwinger faded into the background, in spite of price reductions. The last listing was in 1928, when you could have bought a two-seater for a mere £395.

All in all, about one hundred Redwingers of all types seem to have been made — the four-seater being the most numerous — and in a six-year career it must certainly be called a Victor Wallsgrove project. The sad fact, however, is that by the time the Redwinger was dropped, Wallsgrove had left the company, resigning after the sporting development of the Nine had been allocated to Thomson and Taylors, at Brookland track.

The famous Riley Nine caused a real stir, not only among the motoring pundits, but among rival manufacturers, when it was unveiled in October 1926, on the eve of the opening of the Olympia Motor Show of that year. Perhaps the new vee-12 Daimler Double Six was 'Car of the Year', in technical terms, but that was priced in the rarified atmosphere of all such 50 hp (RAC rating) models; in every other way, the Riley Nine was the most important model at the show.

The March Special (also pictured in the colour section) featured the saloon-length chassis and mechanicals, with a very neat 2+2-seater body style. Engine accessibility was a bit better than it looks.

Although the Nine was all-new, from front dumb-irons to rear number plate, and had several interesting chassis features, it was the advanced engine design which caused such a stir. Although it was a mere 1,087 cc (some say 1,089 cc — but I'll explain this later), and had been designed for a series of family cars, whose prices started at a mere £265, the unit might have been detailed with high power outputs, and motor racing, specifically in mind.

The new engine, *not* the car itself, was vitally important in the long-term Riley scheme of things. Not only did the four-cylinder engine, progressively developed, power Riley cars in every model year from 1927 up to 1938 (when the family-owned company called in the receiver), but a six-cylinder derivative of the design also featured in cars built from 1928 to 1938 as well. In addition, the larger $1\frac{1}{2}$-litre four-cylinder unit first seen in 1934, the 'Big Four' launched in 1937, and the two varieties of vee-8 produced for Riley and Autovia use respectively, all obviously drew on the design and the experience of the Nine for their own particular purposes.

Without the Nine, in other words, the Riley story would have been completely different. Without the Nine, indeed, there might not ever have been a 'Sporting Riley' story to tell.

Although the design of the new Nine was completed during 1925, more than a year was needed to install the tooling necessary to build the new chassis in quantity, and to test every aspect of it. Whereas the old side-valve cars had certainly been designed, and developed, under the control of Harry Rush, the new Nine was a 'Riley family' invention, and the engine was always credited to Percy Riley, with the cylinder head becoming known as the 'PR' head. Stanley Riley developed the chassis.

The original car, *The Autocar* told its readers on 15 October 1926, rode on a channel-section frame, with an 8-foot 10-inch wheelbase, and 4-foot wheel tracks. Their chassis cutaway drawing, by F. Gordon Crosby, showed simple half-elliptic front and rear springing, four-wheel drum brakes (front-wheel brakes were considered necessary on every new model by that time), along with Hartford friction dampers all round.

The two important mechanical innovations were that the gearbox was in unit with the engine (it had been separate on the Side-Valve/Redwinger models, remember), and that the drive to the rear axle was by torque tube transmission, rather than by an open propeller shaft. The gearbox had four forward speeds, and a right-hand gear change whose position could be adjusted to suit the individual driver.

The kernel of the whole design, which was quite unique at the time, and copied by other designers in years to come, was the engine itself. At a time when it was normal for a new family car design to provide a side-valve engine with very inefficient breathing properties, here was a magnificently different layout, not only with overhead valves, but with part-spherical combustions, opposed valves, and *two* camshafts.

Percy Riley's new engine very cleverly provided ideal-looking breathing arrangements without needing to use overhead camshafts, and expensive drive trains to those components. Working outwards from the combustion chamber, he had provided inlet and exhaust valves opposed to each other at an included angle of 90 degrees (each was 45 degrees from the vertical, and the single sparking plug was off-set to one side of the chamber), and had provided each line of valves with its own rocker shaft, reversed rockers, and pushrods, all of which were actuated by a camshaft mounted high up in the crankcase. Each camshaft was supported in two long bearings, and drive from the nose of the crankshaft was by gears.

The cylinder block was separate from the alloy crankcase at first, and made from cast iron, as was the cylinder head. At a very early stage, however, crankcase and block were combined into a single cast iron component. There was cross-flow breathing — the inlet ports being on the right-side of the head, and the exhaust ports being on the left-side (kerb-side for a British market car).

Two important detail features were that oil pressure was by a simple eccentric-tyre pump, that cooling was by thermosyphon to a lofty radiator (there was no water pump), and that the dynamo was mounted on the nose of the crankshaft. A vertical magneto at the front of the engine provided High Tension ignition.

The crankshaft was supported only on two massive main bearings (one next to the clutch, and one immediately behind the camshaft drive gear chain), and the only attempt at counterbalancing was by providing a large weight between Nos 2 and 3 big ends. This, in restrospect, was rather a pity — a properly balanced three-bearing crank would have been much more satisfactory when the racing programme intensified — but in the

Colin Ryder's March Special showing the well-equipped facia. Incidentally, although the car is standing still, the speedometer reads 28 mph!

beginning, when a Nine Monaco produced only about 34 bhp at 4,000 rpm, it was not thought to be important.

The entire engine was mounted by a horizontal cross-member passing through the crankcase between Nos 1 and 2 cylinders, which was then fixed to the chassis longitudinals at each side of the engine bay. Large rubber inserts were fitted between the conically machined lugs of the crankcase, and the collars on the tube, these providing almost the equivalent of a modern flexible engine mounting, although the engine could not move around as much as modern engines do.

At this point I ought to mention the minor disagreement over the engine's actual cylinder capacity. The original descriptions talked of a capacity of 1,087 cc, with a bore and stroke of 60.3 x 95.2 mm. Other sources quoted a capacity of 1,089 cc. In fact Riley, like all other Coventry-based motor car manufacturers, used Imperial measure for their drawings, and the Nine engine nominally had a $2^3/8$-inch bore and a $3^3/4$-inch stroke, with a capacity of 66.452 cu ins. It was as recently as September 1984, in the *Bulletin of the Riley Register,* that a detailed calculation from a Register member produced an exact nominal figure — of 1,088.954 cc. I hope this short review will not result in argument among readers, or Riley enthusiasts — and I intend to assume 1,087 cc (the 'traditional' figure) for the rest of this chapter.

As fitted to the original cars, there was no hint, in the figures, that this was going to be an outstanding power unit in years to come. Magazine road tests of 1927 showed that the Monaco saloon weighed nearly 2,000 lb without passengers. Although it recorded a very creditable fuel consumption figure in the range of 36 and 40 mpg, the Monaco could only reach 56

The input side of this March Special, tucked away under a centre-hinged bonnet, shows twin SU carburettors on the Riley Nine engine.

mph flat out in top gear, and just over 40 mph in third. Where was the sporting potential in this?

The answer, it would transpire, was not only that the power of the willing little engine had to be boosted, but that a lot of weight needed to be taken out of the car, and the aerodynamic drag had to be reduced. The result, seen for the first time in prototype form in August 1927, was the fascinating, low-slung, two-seater Brooklands model. Perhaps, however, we should not use the 'Brooklands' title at first, for the car was originally to be known as the Speed model when it went on sale in 1928.

Although a great deal is known about the engineering of the Brooklands Nine, and about their history, the origins of the cars are still not entirely clear. Perhaps the best summary of the car's rather complex beginnings come from Dr. Birmingham:

'J.G. Parry-Thomas, just before his death in 1927, was engaged in developing the Nine, and his experiments were carried on by Reid Railton, who was connected with the Thomas Inventions Development Co. Ltd, at Brooklands. The experiments were aimed at producing a racing Riley Nine with a view to the production of a marketable sports model. The car was actually built by Thomson & Taylor Ltd.'

So far, so good, but perhaps this excellent description should be enlarged a little further, after we consider Riley's own commercial position in 1926 and 1927. Getting the all-new Nine into series production was a very big task, and there is evidence that the initial launch was premature, so that the design could, at least, be displayed at the Olympia Motor Show of 1926.

Writing about these interesting events, many years later, Montague Tombs, long-serving Technical Editor of *The Autocar,* who spent most of his time in and around Coventry between the wars, pointed out that his description of the chassis, in October 1926, made no mention of the coachwork to be used, and that the Monaco saloon did not actually go on sale until June 1927, eight months later.

The editor of *Motor Sport,* William Boddy, had this thoughtful comment to make in the issue of March 1978:

'It can be argued that with three new body styles in the offing and the original chassis requiring a slightly lower compression ratio, a steady bearing for its propeller shaft, alterations to the wheels and brakes, and the engine a one-piece block and crankcase, they would have little time for turning the great little Nine into a sports model. Riley's had, in addition, the producing facilities to sort out, the first 1,000 production Nines having been made in their engine factory. Thus it is quite possible that they sub-contracted the sports car ambition.'

In fact there appears to be little doubt about this, as technical analyses of the first prototype Speed Models, published in August 1927, make clear. Parry Thomas, by that time at the very height of his fame, had progressed from designing the magnificent Leyland Eight, to taking an interest in the Arab sports car project (where his design assistant was Reid Railton), and had founded the Thomas Inventions Development Co. Ltd., with workshops inside the concrete bowl of the Brooklands race track, in Surrey. There he not only continued to develop his own competition cars, including the gargantuan 'Babs', but undertook design and development work for other companies.

In March 1927, Thomas went off to Pendine Sands, in South Wales, to attempt to break the Land Speed Record in 'Babs', but the car crashed at high speed, and the larger-than-life Welshman was killed instantly. One result of this was that Reid Railton carried on the work of the company for a time (which included the evolution of the Nine Speed Model), until both were eventually absorbed into the Thomson and Taylor organisation, which was an even better known race-tuning concern, and which was also based inside the Brooklands track.

The project work was made public in August 1927, when the first (and, so far, only) car was shown off. At that stage very little running had taken place, and although the car was quite startlingly low, its chassis was entirely different from that which would be used on a production basis.

On the prototype, the chassis frame of a standard Riley Nine model had been cut and modified at the rear, which reduced the wheelbase from the 8 ft 10.5 ins of a Monaco to only 7 ft 7.5 ins — a reduction of 15 inches. The front half of the resulting frame was absolutely standard, but the newly-fabricated rear end swept sharply inwards over the top of the rear

The exhaust side of the March Special, in this case, had a free-flow exhaust system, but as with all Rileys I'm sure you could have had it otherwise, to order! The Klaxon horn is almost as big as the dynamo!

axle. The rear springs, slung under the frame of the standard car, were now arranged to be outside the new frame, with new pads to the rear axle to suit. Front axles, springs and damper positions, plus the steering layout, were all 'as standard'.

Allied to this, Parry-Thomas, and later Railton, had reshuffled the seating so that the two seats were now positioned inside the line of the side members, and dropped so far down that the driver could brush his hand on to the ground outside the starkly-trimmed, two-seater bodywork. There was a new, small, and much lowered radiator position, the whole car being no more than 36 inches high at the scuttle. There was a full length air-smoothing undershield.

I ought to state, right away, that this was not the form in which the new Speed Model was eventually put on sale. Production cars, of which Thomson & Taylor built the first small batch at Brooklands, and of which an example was displayed as a last-minute Olympia 'show surprise', had a completely new, specially-designed, frame, whose side members dipped smartly down behind the line of the front axle, swept smoothly under a modified two-seater body style, and ran *under* the line of the back axle. The wheelbase had been rounded up to 8 feet.

This car was put on sale as the Speed Model, for £395 (which compared with the £298 asked for an open four-seater Nine of the period), in which guise it had a sleek two-door body style with a pointed tail. There were cycle-type front wings on the very first show car, which also did not have a windscreen of any type; so-called 'production cars' (for production was always limited) usually had a one or two-piece full-width screen, and a rather skimpy fold-down hood, while the front wings swept back in a straight line from the top of the front wings to a fixing point on the frame, near the trailing edge of the bonnet.

Mechanically, the Brooklands Speed Model (and I now propose to abbreviate that title merely to 'Brooklands', as everyone else seems to do) was closely based on the current Nine family car design. Most of the work had gone into the tuning of the engine. Not only was the engine fitted with twin carburettors (SUs, or Solex), and an efficient-looking exhaust manifold, but there was a much-modified camshaft profile, which offered 45 degrees of overlap around Top Dead Centre; in particular, the inlet valve began to open 20 degrees before Top Dead Centre, instead of at Top Dead Centre in the touring engines. There was water-pump assisted cooling, and H.T. ignition was supplied by a magneto. Whereas Riley power outputs are generally not known, in this case a figure of 50 bhp at 5,000 rpm is usually quoted.

Behind the engine there was the usual type of four-speed transmission; earlier cars had a long central lever, but later a neat, short-throw, remote control change was usually incorporated. Torque tube drive to the spiral bevel back axle was retained, and the usual final drive ratio supplied was 4.77:1 (it was 5.25:1 on the saloons). Early cars had five bolt-fixing wire

spoke wheels, and 10-inch brake drums, but these would both be upgraded in the years which followed. Operation was by cables and rods, like that of the ordinary Nines, and it soon became apparent that a lack of brakes would eventually be the competition car's weak spot.

The whole car was tiny, and light, which allowed Riley to guarantee a top speed of at least 80 mph in road-equipped form. The original prototype, when tried out at Brooklands without a screen or any other drag-raising fittings, was timed at better than 90 mph, and in its first race (with Railton himself behind the wheel) it lapped at 98.62 mph, taking the handicappers completely by surprise!

The story of the Brooklands is really one of a limited-production car which did so very well in motor sport — especially in racing (see Chapter V) — but which was nevertheless a practical, if not very sybaritically-equipped, road car as well. It could not entirely have been at a whim that Riley made sure that the famous S.C.H. 'Sammy' Davis used a Brooklands on the Lands End Trial, gaining a Gold award, for an unpenalised run, in spite of the very limited ground clearance offered by this model.

As with the Redwinger model that it immediately displaced, the

Brooklands was not, by any means, a mass-production machine, and after sales began, haltingly, in 1928, Rileys made little apparent attempt to promote its use as a road car. With the wonderful aid of hindsight, it is possible to see that there was some interest in it during 1928, but that once the smooth new six-cylinder cars had appeared at the end of that year, then sales and promotion staff had more pressing things to do.

Although the last 'works' Brooklands racers were built up in 1932, Richard Wills, who owns the final car (which is pictured in the colour section) states that no chassis were built after the end of 1930. Certainly by 1931 and 1932, when British car sales were diving into the slump of the Depression, there was little demand for such frivolities, particularly as the price of the road car had risen to £420, or even to £475 for the 'Plus' derivative, which had the four Amal engine, and other details.

How many were made? No one knows, for sure. It is estimated that about 30,000 Nines of all types were made in rather more than ten years, of which the saloons accounted for the vast majority, and that between 100 and 200 Brooklands were made.

In the early 1930s, therefore, there was no truly sporting Nine on sale, nor indeed would there be one from the factory until the arrival of the Imp

The Imp, from this angle and others, shows a strong similarity to the style of the MPH, which was launched in the same year. Although there were some common panels, there was a startling difference in performance. Who cares if the following cars got drenched in spray from the exposed rear wheels?

in 1934. However, in the interim, the Riley-based March Special was launched in September 1932, filled the gap for rather more than a year, and is now a well-thought-of, and rare, machine.

The basis of the March Special was the rolling chassis of the standard Riley Nine, with the 8 foot 10.5-inch wheelbase, and bolt-on wire-spoke wheels. The project had been developed by Messrs Kevill-Davies and March Ltd., of London, a motoring business of which the most famous personality was 'Freddie' March (more correctly the Earl of March), who later became the Duke of Richmond & Gordon (and, of course, thus became the 'landlord' of the Goodwood racing circuit).

The Earl of March had already made quite a name as a young racing driver in British events. This was by no means his first bright idea, and it carried coachwork produced by John Charles & Sons at Kew, in south-west London. It was a close-coupled four-seater tourer looking like several other British sports cars of the period, featuring cutaway doors, and carrying twin spare wheels at the back of the body shell.

When it was announced, there were promises of March Special coachwork on the four-cylinder *and* the six-cylinder chassis, though March Special owner Colin Ryder has no conclusive evidence that any six-cylinder cars were ever completed. *The Autocar* quoted a price of £325 for the first cars, but the production cars were sold for £335.

Having seen what was proposed, Riley took the March Special on board, and included it in their catalogues for the 1933 model year; the cars were sold through the Riley dealer network, and since the rolling chassis was standard, service and maintenance was not a problem. Rolling chassis were supplied to Kew for completion, then returned to the dealers' network, and it is doubtful that K-D & M saw many of them at their Bruton Street premises.

All the cars were based on 1933 model year chassis (for they were not listed for 1934), and it seems that about 60 March Specials were built. Perhaps it is heresy, but I find the March Special as attractive a style, if not more so, than the Lynx which ran for several years as a Riley-built car.

The definitive sporting Nine, however, was certainly the Imp, although even this name suffered a false start, when exhibited at Olympia in the autumn of 1933 with a cramped 2 + 2-seater body style not unlike that of the superseded March Special at the front, but with a rather squared up tail. It did not go into production.

The *real* Imp made its bow, very modestly indeed as far as press announcements were concerned. It is quite typical of Riley's scandalously casual method of marketing sports cars that early two-seater Imps took part in the London-Edinburgh trial, and the Scottish Rally, in the spring of 1934, but that no technical description of the Imp was ever published in influential magazines where possible customers might have been expected to look.

Yet, if only Victor Riley and his team had troubled to look, here was a

No problem in getting at the spare wheel of the Imp, which was held down by a central clamp. The petrol tank was tucked away underneath it.

Below left: This front end detail is of an Imp, but can't you see the similarity to other Rileys of the period?

Below: Everything about the Imp was so absolutely right for the mid-1930s period – what a pity Riley never properly promoted it, nor gave it enough power to do a proper job.

sensationally beautiful sports car, that should have sold in much greater quantities than it did. Not only did the new car look good, but it was also based on a racing Riley chassis which had already made a name for itself.

The story, told in more detail in the next chapter, begins with the Brooklands Six of 1932, which had a completely new chassis, one which had substantial stiff side members, and which swept under the line of the back axle. In Brooklands Six form, its wheelbase was 9 feet, though the six-cylinder cars which evolved from that car, and the MPH road car which followed, all used an 8 foot 1.5-inch wheelbase. The Imp was to use a further shortened version of the same frame, with a 7 foot 6-inch wheelbase — this, incidentally, being even shorter than that of the Brooklands Nine, and being the shortest of any sporting Riley covered in this book.

First, however, I ought to consider the styling of the Imp (and its very close relative, the MPH, which is covered in the next chapter), look around the world of European sports car motoring of the period, and draw in two very well-known names indeed — Donald Healey and Alfa Romeo.

Firstly, I note that Alfa Romeo was the world's most successful builder of Supercars in the early 1930s, and that every other European manufacturer was either jealous of their sporting success, or interested in copying what they were doing — one way or another. Although no-one could match their magnificent supercharged engines, there was always the chance that the styling of their rakish two-seaters could be studied, and used, for inspiration. The 1750s were already well-known in the UK by the early 1930s, and the first of the eight-cylinder 8C2300s were imported before the end of 1931.

Secondly, there was Donald Healey, a young Cornishman whose family home was in Perranporth, who soon became involved in the motor trade, and in motor sport, who became a successful rally driver by the end of the 1920s, and who achieved lasting glory in British sporting history by winning the Monte Carlo rally of 1931, driving a 4$\frac{1}{2}$-litre Invicta.

He soon became a Riley 'works' driver too, but by 1933 he had actually moved from Cornwall, to live in digs in Barford, near Warwick, and was working as a development engineer in the experimental department at Rileys. In the summer of that year he drove a Brooklands Nine (KV 5392 — the car owned today by Richard Wills) to an unpenalised *Coupe des Glaciers* award in the International Alpine Trial. However, this was not to be a long stay at Riley, for in September 1933 Donald Healey moved on, to become experimental manager at Triumph (another Coventry concern), and shortly become that company's technical director.

There is no doubt in my mind that Donald Healey was drafted in to Riley, to work on new sports cars, for both the Imp and the MPH must have been taking shape during his sojourn with the Riley company. It is also beyond doubt that Healey had some influence on the shaping of these two cars, for his admiration for the Alfa Romeo style was well-known. If any further proof is needed, look at the car which Healey inspired as soon as he became established at Triumph — the eight-cylinder supercharged Dolomite — at its styling, and at certain similarities to the Imp/MPH!

The Imp's frame, in the context of the 1.1-litre engine (and about 40 bhp), which had to propel it, was really far too solid, and throughout its life the car suffered the handicap of carrying too much weight — and of the potential clientele knowing that this was so. Incidentally it also had much in common with the frame of the Monaco saloon.

Students of Riley industrial archaeology found much in the Imp with which they were already familiar in other models, including the 1,087-cc engine, the usual 3 foot 11.75-inch wheel tracks, and the use of 5.25:1 final drive. The 'usual' 19-inch centre-lock wire wheels were used, along with the typical continuous cable braking installation. The engine had twin SU carburettors, coil and distributor ignition, and a camshaft profile developed from the latest sporting practice.

In sporting terms, the major change was in the transmission, where the Imp was offered either with the usual type of Nine-based four-speed manual gearbox, or as an option with the ENV pre-selector transmission which had just become available on Nines for the 1934 season. The pity of it was that although the pre-selector change made driving simple and pleasurable, it also took the edge off the already limited performance of the Imp.

About the styling, however, there could be no doubt. Like the MPH, the Imp was clearly shaped with an eye to what was most fashionable in

The packed instrument panel layout of John Gathercole's Imp, is remarkably similar to that of the MPH (introduced the same year), and the Sprite (introduced less than two years later). See pages 42 and 54 to compare notes.

The Ulster Imp was a short-lived successor to the racing Brooklands Nine, introduced in 1934 and priced at £450. It was shorter, but no lighter, than the Brooklands, and rode on the latest, more solid, chassis.

The Ulster Imp's 1,087 cc engine filled its small compartment — and when new probably never looked anything like as smart as this!

Italy, at the time. Unlike the old Brooklands, the Imp was a much more 'integrated' car (in artistic terms), with a more civilised driving compartment. The front and rear wings flowed beautifully along the flanks, there was a fold-down windscreen, usually with twin aero screens behind it, and a smoothly shaped tail with the spare wheel mounted at an angle. The rear wings ended in a cheeky high kick, allowing rain to spew unhindered on to the following cars.

Although the Imps made their debut in spring, they were not really available for general sale until the autumn of 1934, and at this point the price was £298 for an Imp with manual transmission, or £325 if the pre-selector transmission was specified. As it happens, and in spite of the power-sapping qualities, it seems that the vast majority of all Imps were fitted with pre-selector transmission.

Let us also be frank about one Imp feature, which seems ever more ludicrous today — the cockpit was very small indeed, and there was really no question of tall, or bulky, drivers ever getting comfortable. As John Gathercole wrote in the *Bulletin* of March 1984:

'Sidescreens were available, though not many have them. Certainly doors were drilled to taken them. But as most conventionally built adults (with arms and things) overflow the cockpit in all directions, their use is limited . . . The hood is a different matter. It fits well, and the car can press on when wearing it.'

Even so, for all that it was a very attractive-looking car with good roadmanners, the Imp was not very fast, and this may explain why Riley never made a fuss about it, nor lent out a demonstrator for press road testing. The car was in production until the end of 1935 model year (i.e

Inlet detail of the twin SU Nine engine, dating from mid-1930s. Air cleaners? Don't be facetious — there wasn't space under the bonnet in any case.

The exhaust manifold of the Ulster Imp was about as efficiently formed as possible, by mid-1930s racing knowledge standards.

Driver's eye view (almost) of the front end of the Ulster Imp — there is almost a touch of ERA (or, shall we say, White Riley?) about it.

until the summer of 1935), and in perhaps only a year as a series production machine, between 150 and 200 cars were built.

In the autumn of 1935, however, there was a further change in Riley's sports car line-up, when both the Imp and the MPH (see Chapter III) were dropped, to make way for the Sprite. The new model, though closely linked

This Ulster Imp hides nothing — the gearbox and its remote linkage being in full view, and *very* close to the driver's legs.

to the MPH and the Imp in general layout, had an entirely different engine, and was a direct spin-off from the 1935 Riley racing sports car.

In the autumn of 1934, for the first time since 1928, Riley announced a new engine design. This was a $1\frac{1}{2}$-litre four-cylinder unit which had a very familiar-looking twin high camshaft/pushrod overhead valve gear layout, but was much larger, and completely different in every detail, from that of the Nine.

However Riley made what, to some historians, was a very strange decision. Instead of neatly phasing out the older six-cylinder engines, to make way for the new (and, presumably, cheaper to make) $1\frac{1}{2}$-litre 'four', they elected to keep both engines in production, effectively competing with each other. This must have made production planning, showroom displays, and advertising, that much more difficult to cope with — and it was a situation which was to persist until 1938.

Not only with the production cars, but with the race cars too, there was a clash between the two types. The latest racing Rileys, produced in 1935, were called TT Sprites. In the next two years, depending on the cars used, on the regulations which applied to the races and — one suspects — on the whim of management, TT Sprites sometimes raced with the 'six', and sometimes with the 'four'!

The Sprite production car, however, slipped into the Riley model range with absolutely no fuss. Indeed, this seems to have been another of those occasions where Riley went out of their way to make sure the public were *not* informed about a new sports car. There were no pictures in the motoring press, no technical analyses, and no road tests until 1937, when

Alloy back plates on the front drums of the Ulster Imp. Braking by cable, of course.

The Autocar at last got its hands on a car, perhaps because its Managing Editor's son had recently bought one of his own!

In broad terms, but by no means just this in detail, the Sprite was effectively an engine transplant into the MPH's structure, with some style changes to make the transformation more obvious. The very first Sprite prototype (AKV 218, which still exists) was produced by modifying an MPH chassis, fitting Girling rod-actuated brakes, inserting a specially-tuned 1½-litre 12/4 four-cylinder engine, and retaining the traditional nose. That car, driven by W.K. Elliott, won its class in the Scottish SCC's Edinburgh Half-Day Trial even before it was publically launched.

The production car, however, retained the basic layout of the MPH'S chassis, and the 3 foot 11.75-inch wheel tracks, but had much stiffening and the side members were boxed from front to rear of the frame. The 19-inch wheels, and tyres, too, were all like those of the MPH, but the continuous cable braking system had been cast out, to be replaced by a much more satisfactory, and practical, Girling mechanical rod installation. As ever, there were half-elliptic leaf springs at front and rear, plus friction dampers, while the MPH-derived chassis frame passed underneath the line of the back axle.

The engine's capacity was 1,496 cc and used the 'classic British'

The Lynx was an under-estimated little car, let down (like the Imp) by being too heavy for its engine. Here is an example in the Lands End Trial in 1935.

dimensions of a 69-mm bore and a 100-mm stroke (which produced an RAC horsepower rating of 11.9, and which seemed to crop up on so many other engines in the inter-war period). In general layout it was similar to Percy Riley's famous Nine, with two camshafts — one on each side of the cylinder block — each driving pushrods and reversed rockers, to valves in the cylinder head. However, unlike the little Nine, the 1½-litre unit had a three-bearing crankshaft, which gave it better reserves of strength and rigidity.

The combustion chamber was part spherical, and the valves were opposed to each other, at an included angle of 90 degrees, with a single sparking plug offset from the crown of the chamber. There were individual inlet and exhaust ports, and naturally there was 'cross-flow' breathing, with the exhaust system on the left side, and the carburation on the right side of the unit.

On the 1½-litre units used in the saloon cars, there was elaborate hot-spotting (of the inlet manifold by hot exhaust gases) provided by passages through the cylinder blocks, and head, and the standard tune featured a single Zenith carburettor. For the Sprite application, the hot spotting tubes were not provided, twin SU carburettors were fitted, and more sporty camshaft profiles were used. Saloons had coil ignition, but the

Below left: The Lynx style was made for several years – here is a latter-day example, fitted with the 1½-litre 12/4 engine. Is it not sporting enough for you?

Below: The Sprite of 1935-8 was the only Riley sports car to have this 'waterfall' type radiator grille. The classic style was also available, and some customers ordered it. This particular car has used both types in recent years.

Sprites had a magneto system, thought to be more suitable for the sporting purpose. All in all, the 1½-litre 'four' was perhaps a little less powerful than the MPH unit which it superseded, but by most mid-1930s standards the Sprite was still a spirited car.

Like the MPH, the Sprite was available with manual transmission, or the pre-selector gears. The manual box, even in 1935, was still related to that of the Brooklands Nine, and had a Brooklands-type remote control. However, not many Sprite road cars appear to have had this transmission, the majority all having the pre-selector gears, with four forward speeds, and with the selector lever to the right of the steering column. As usual, there was torque-tube drive to the spiral bevel back axle, the final drive ratio being 5.22:1 in both cases.

The body, according to owners, and Riley fanatics, was significantly altered in several respects from that of the MPH. It was slightly more roomy (and longer) at the rear, while the wing lines were, of course, completely different, particularly at the rear where the rear tyres were much more completely covered. The cockpit was still very restricted,

This car is a Sprite, but all the Imp/MPH/Sprite generation had a very cramped cockpit. It helped to be small if you were a Riley sports car customer.

The windscreen of the Sprite could be folded forward, and many spent the summer months in this condition. In such cases, an aero screen was enough to keep draughts (and flies) out of the driver's face.

To stow the aero screens on a Sprite, they could be fitted into slots on the scuttle, behind the engine bay, and above the foot wells.

especially for drivers wearing bulky winter clothing (no heater, remember . . .), thought the control layout was virtually the same.

At the front, the car was normally supplied with a new type of 'waterfall' or 'fencer's mask' radiator grille thought to be boldly modern for the period, and therefore almost certain to offend Riley traditionalists! Riley's body engineers had foreseen this reaction, and arranged things so that the car could be (and sometimes was) supplied with the traditional, MPH-type, radiator grille and style. It was quite easy to convert a Sprite from one front style to the other.

When the car was announced (or, rather, when it slipped modestly into the model range for 1936), it was priced at £425 with the 1½-litre four-cylinder engine. At first there was also supposedly an alternative engine — the long-established six-cylinder unit, in 2-litre form — but this £550 version of the Sprite seems to have existed only on paper, and none seem to have been built, not even as experimental vehicles.

The Sprite, like the MPH before it, had a hard time in making its name, though it was catalogued until 1938. Riley advertising spoke of the car's appeal to 'Motorists who still regard motoring as a sport. Men who drive through the night seeking gold medals and revel in the almost unclimbable mountain tracks. Men and women whose cars must not only look fast, but be fast. Men to whom racing, hill-climbs and trials are the most fascinating things in life.' Maybe — the problem was that there were very few of these people.

Estimates of numbers built *can* only be informed guesses, for reasons already made clear. However, Vernon Barker's 1977 estimates published in the *Register Bulletin* (and quoted here, with grateful acknowledgement) suggested between 20 and 30 cars made in 1936 model year, 25 to 35 in 1937 model year, and three to five in the 1938 season. Work it out how you will — but it seems that between 50 and 70 Sprites *may* have been built. In 1971, certainly, a list of no fewer than 41 mainly-British Sprites was published in the Bulletin, and this was always acknowledged to be incomplete.

Although the Sprite's special-series engine was offered in other Riley cars of the 1935-9 period — Lynx and Kestrel models being particularly pleasing — this was Riley's final fling with two-seater sports cars. Hit hard by cars like the SS100 (which was no more expensive, even in $3^{1}/_{2}$-litre/125 bhp form), the Sprite had virtually faded out, even before the company called in the receiver early in 1938. Considering the successes notched up by the 'works' TT Sprites of the period, this is surprising, and must have been a great disappointment to the company.

Heaton-Fairclough's Sprite competing in an MCC trial in the late 1930s — the natural habitat for this car. Note the extra fitting on this car: the auxiliary lamp squeezed in behind the grille mesh.

III
Sporting Rileys: The 'Sixes'

Riley was never a rich company, though the way money was spent at times made one think it was. There were times of real prosperity, of course, but there was never a load of money washing around, to be squandered on unnecessary engineering projects. Riley was never large enough — they never made enough cars, or enough money — to justify the design and manufacture of several different engine families in quick succession. That they did so, in the mid 1930s, is one good reason why they eventually had to call in the receiver in 1938!

In the later 1920s, however, this logic explains why they chose to follow up the neat and efficient little four-cylinder Nine engine with a straight-six that had been developed directly from it. Look at the engine of a Brooklands, then look at the engine of an MPH, and the blood-relationship is clear; the two units shared many common components, and much of the machining facilities in Riley's Coventry factories. Most observers with engineering training would agree that the two units were certainly conceived by Percy Riley, if not designed in detail, at the same time.

Now — and if you are not a lover of fine cars, vintage, thoroughbred *or* modern, you will never understand my next statement — there is nothing quite so sensually appealing to a driver as a really pleasing straight-six-cylinder engine. If properly designed, balanced, and built, there is no smoother type of engine in the business. Certainly I have never met an enthusiast driver who does not enjoy motoring behind a silky-smooth 'six'.

Visually, too, a straight-six looks more impressive than almost every other type. It is certainly more purposeful than a 'four', and altogether more elegant in its mechanical architecture than a vee-eight — or a vee-six for that matter. I throw in the latter comparison, not because there were such things in the British motor industry of the 1920s, but because much of my modern-car motoring is vee-six powered. There may be a lot of power and torque up front (fuel injection helps see to that), but it simply doesn't feel the same.

This explains the thinking behind Riley's new-product strategy in the late 1920s. Having surprised, and delighted, the British motoring world in 1926, Percy Riley was encouraged to do even better next time around, even though the next phase could not be introduced at once. For 1927 the Riley range included two model families: the new Nine, which was certainly 'As Modern as the Hour', and the side-valve Twelve, which was beginning to look distinctly old-fashioned.

The Twelve's engine, after all, had its design roots in the original post-war car of 1919, and not even the Redwinger's reputation, and the short-lived showing of a supercharged short-chassis derivative, could do much to freshen up its image.

Behind the scenes in Coventry, however, work was already going ahead to change all that, to run down the Twelve, and to bring in another new family of cars. As so many other British motor car manufacturers did in the 1920s and 1930s, Riley were preparing to evolve a complete engine family from a single basic design. Even though there was no evidence of automation in the factories (Morris Engines, also in Coventry, were the pioneers in this field), it still made sense to commonise one engine with another, as far as was feasible and practical.

For Riley, the obvious and logical thing to do was to produce a new straight-six engine which used as much as possible of the basic design of

The early-1930s style of Alfa Romeo (this is an eight-cylinder Monza) definitely influenced the shape of the MPH which was conceived a couple of years later.

The MPH was an out-and-out sports car, and looked it, but the six-cylinder engine was originally used in humble saloons like this Lincock first seen in 1932.

the four-cylinder Nine. Perhaps it is simplistic to suggest that the original six-cylinder Riley was really no more than one-and-a-half Nines, but that was the impression (visually and technically) given by the chosen new design. Many components — valve gear, camshaft drive and electrical details, pistons, connecting rods and the like, were all the same, while the two units also shared the same bore, stroke, and breathing arrangements.

As before, Percy Riley was responsible for the design layout of the engine, though he certainly did not produce all the drawings, single-handed. It was not single-minded genius which produced such an engine, just sheer practical Coventry common sense, the support of the complete Riley family, and speedy development by an experienced workforce.

The new engine, and a chassis to go with it, were unveiled in September 1928, and *The Autocar* greeted it like this:

'Certain characteristics, as original as they are concisely practical,

The six-cylinder engine was announced in 1928, when it had a single carburettor, and looked less tidy than this early-1930s Lincock example. The MPH (and, eventually, the ERA) was developed from it.

have caused the Riley Nine to be regarded as the most advanced design of British-built small car on the market . . . Now the makers have completed the task of giving the Nine a larger brother, and are placing on the market a five-seater of similar characteristics, but with a six-cylinder engine . . .

. . . Broadly, the six-cylinder engine has a similar layout to that of the four-cylinder 9 hp, in as much as the bore and the stroke are the same, and also the cylinder design. Hemispherical cylinder heads are

Exhaust side of the six-cylinder 12/6 saloon car version of the engine later much-tuned for use in the MPH.

used [the writer of this description actually meant to say 'combustion
chambers', not 'heads'!] and in them the valves are set at 90 degrees,
with the sparking plugs vertical but slightly off centre. Both the inlet
and exhaust ports run straight out of the casting and are machined . . .'

To Riley's credit, they did not try to bluff the public, by suggesting
that here was an entirely new engine design, unconnected with any other.
Other firms, throughout the British motor industry, were by no means as
honest in this period.

Visually, the two engines — the four-cylinder and six-cylinder — were
uncannily similar, even though the new 'six' had coil ignition instead of the
Nine's magneto type, for there was that characteristic cross-shaft fixing
arrangement through the block/crankcase for the front engine mountings,
between the line of the first and second cylinder barrels, while the gear
train needed to drive the two camshafts (one at each side of the cylinder
block), and the fixing of the dynamo end on to the front of the crankshaft,
were all the same.

When the car was announced, and named Stelvio, the carburettor
arrangement — single or twin — had not finally been settled, but
production cars were equipped with a single SU. At first cooling was by
thermosyphon, but a pump-and-thermostat design change was already
being considered.

The big difference, of course, was in the layout of the crankshaft. On
the four-cylinder Nine, of course, there had been a very stiff, single-plane,
crankshaft, supported on only two main bearings. The new six-cylinder
crank was much more complex in its design, and needed extra support in
the centre, for it was naturally considerably longer and more heavily
stressed.

Mathematicians will tell you that at least four, and preferably seven,
crankshaft main bearings are needed for a straight 'six'. No doubt Percy
Riley knew all about this — but decided to choose something different.
Instead, he provided just three main bearings — one at each end, of course,
and a large-diameter centre bearing between cylinders three and four.

The Autocar, probably taking its text from Riley's own press release on
the subject, wrote that:

'In this stiff [cylinder block/crankcase] casting the crankshaft is
carried in three bearings, and these bearings should be amply
sufficient, for the overall length of the crankshaft is not great, while
the shaft is massive, and has circular webs. It is threaded into its
bearings from the back of the crankcase, hence the centre bearing is of
considerable diameter. It has very wide flanges, and provides a
particularly solid abutment for the endwise location of the shaft.
Incidentally, all the crankshaft and big end bearings are pressure
lubricated through ways drilled in the shaft; there are no oil pipes.'

These original six-cylinder engines, of course, had three plain bearings, the centre one being of no less than 3³/₄ inches diameter (to allow the crankshaft to be threaded through, not because the engine stresses required such a size). It was not until 1932, when the first sporting six-cylinder Riley appeared, that the now-discredited water-cooled bearing would put in an appearance.

The original 'six' of 1928, therefore, had an RAC horsepower rating of 13.5, so Riley called it a 6/14 hp unit (or alternatively a 14/50 hp — the second figure relating to the claimed peak power output), because it had the same bore and stroke as the four-cylinder Nine. This gave it a swept volume of 1,633 cc. Clearly, at that stage, Riley did not even consider using this engine for competition purposes, as the appropriate class limits were 1,500 cc, or 2,000 cc.

In the years to come, other capacities would be developed, not only by Riley but most notably by ERA (see Chapter X where ERA used the 'six' as the basis for their racing engine). In this application, engines as small as 1,088 cc and as large as 1,980 cc would eventually be used.

I have concentrated my attention on the engine of the Stelvio and Deauville models, so far, because the rest of the car's mechanical specification was entirely predictable. The gearbox was the 'Silent Third' type, as used in the Riley, with central change and a long gear lever incorporating a visible 'gate' for selection purposes, while the spiral bevel differential was of the same basic design.

The original cars ran on a heavy chassis, with a wheelbase of no less

Most Riley enthusiasts think the MPH was the most beautiful of all between-wars Rileys. This view of a well-known car backs up this opinion, surely?

Show me a design or styling detail out of place on this MPH — a luscious car in all respects.

than 10 feet and wheel tracks of 4 feet 8 inches — which meant that the new six-cylinder engine had to work very hard to provide adequate performance. The gearing was dreadfully low, as with other 'small Sixes' of the period — the final drive ratio being no less than 5.75:1. The 'Light Six' models, which arrived a year later, and from which the Alpine saloons were soon to be derived, were considerably smaller, and lighter, running on a 9 foot 6-inch wheelbase chassis with 4-foot wheel tracks, which was effectively a lengthened version of the Nine's Mark IV chassis and suspension.

Such cars even carried coachwork clearly derived from those of the Nines — they were the same aft of the scuttle, for all the wheelbase 'stretch' was up front, to accommodate the longer engine — and the engines were beginning to look distinctly sporting, for the water pump method of cooling had been standardised, and *The Autocar* of 11 October 1929 carried a neat chassis drawing showing a twin SU carburettor installation.

Basic engine, gearbox, torque tube transmission, axles, wheels and suspension were all clearly those of the Nine (or developed from them), and Riley were evidently milking their basic 'design-Meccano' philosophy as hard as they could, to produce many different models, in what were becoming troubled economic times for the British motor industry.

One Riley peculiarity (or, shall I diplomatically say, 'feature') evident on these cars was the braking installation, which relied on monstrously long cables which completed a tortuous path between the front and rear of the car, and included pulleys, adjustments, and all manner of detail which was simply asking to become rusted up, or corroded, in the years which followed. Riley, unlike Triumph, were still not at all convinced that hydraulic brakes were the answer.

But still there was nothing remotely 'sporting' about these six-cylinder Rileys. Although the company was busily developing a 'works' competition team of Brooklands Nines, and there was a considerable amount of engine-tuning expertise being acquired, which could be applied to the four-cylinder *and* the six-cylinder engines, Riley continued to build a multiplicity of touring cars, most with saloon car coachwork, a few with open tourer styles. Even by 1930/31, when the Stelvio had the twin SU engine, road tests showed it to be capable of only 67 mph, with a fuel consumption of about 20 mpg. Weight, as with most Rileys of this period, was a problem, and hit hard at performance and fuel efficiency.

All that began to change in 1932, when the first of the ultra-sporting 'Sixes' — the Brooklands Six — was unveiled. The original design, shown in May 1932, was different in many ways from the series-production Sixes, though it used the entire engine/drive line as the basis for power and race-tuning, and was said to be loosely derived from the Alpine Six tourer.

The first sentence in *The Autocar's* detailed technical analysis said that: 'After examining a batch of the new Riley six-cylinder Brooklands models in the course of construction, an observer cannot help admiring the individuality of the design . . .' — which pre-supposes that Riley were interested in selling the cars to the public.

The fact is, however, that only two Brooklands Sixes were ever built — these being the first of several six-cylinder sporting Rileys which were commercial failures. The price quoted at this time was £595, which was a considerable sum for the period, when Britain's motor industry was trying to fight its way out of the economic blizzard we now call the Depression.

The car revealed at first was a pure competition car, but its chassis layout is so significant to Riley's sporting future that it ought to be described here. The next generation of racing Rileys, the 1933 TT Sixes, evolved from that layout, the MPH road car used the same frames as those cars, as did the famous 'White Riley', while the Sprite similarly evolved from the MPH.

The stout chassis frame had channel section side members, gently curving over the forged front axle beam, and slipping neatly under the line of the back axle. There was a tubular cross-member between the front of the dumb irons, a second cross-tube behind the line of the front axle (and supporting the radiator mounts), a large tubular cross-member under the rear of the gearbox, a fourth cross-tube joining the front rear leaf spring brackets, and a fifth cross-tube at the very tail.

Front and rear suspension was by sturdy half-elliptic leaf springs, with no extra axle location, and damping was by Duplex Andre lever arm shock absorbers. The front springs were under the line of the chassis side members, the much longer rear springs not only being slung under the axle casing, but also mounted outside the chassis side members to give a wide (anti-roll) spring base.

The steering was of the usual Riley type, with the steering box mounted inboard of the right-side chassis member, and connected to the front end by a long drag link. There were 19-inch centre lock wire spoke wheels, with a 3.5-inch rim width; on the MPH, and on the Sprite, this rim width would be reduced to a more conventional (by the standards of the day) 3 inches. The brakes, with racing in mind, were quite enormous, and had 13-inch drums, all controlled by the usual type of continuous cable Riley system.

Because the Brooklands Six had been evolved purely with motor sport in mind, it had been necessary to reduce the size of the engine to bring it below the 1,500 cc class limit. This had been done by reducing the cylinder bore from the 60.3 mm of the standard six-cylinder engine, to 57.546 mm, without change to the crankshaft or to the 95.25 mm stroke; the capacity accordingly worked out at 1,486 cc.

57.546 mm? Yes, it's a very odd, and precise, dimension indeed,

Some MPHs had small headlamps to cut wind resistance, some (like this car) had larger ones to give better illumination. The lens mesh was purely functional, to ward off stones.

especially when one realises that it is also a very odd imperial dimension (2.266 inches) as well; for those who cared, the RAC Rating had been reduced to 12.3. Don't expect me to explain — Riley never did! Incidentally this was not the last of the strange swept volume figures to be evolved for the six-cylinder engine, for other Riley cars eventually used 1,458 cc (12 hp RAC rating) and 1,726 cc (14.3 hp RAC rating).

The basic design of the engine needed no change, although the obvious visual change was the use of three horizontal SU carburettors and a more efficient exhaust system. Hidden away were large inlet valves, and more ambitious camshaft timing, with 60 degrees of overlap, this being even more than normally specified in the Brooklands Nine four-cylinder engine.

The important internal change was to the crankshaft's centre main bearing which on this car was now given a slim water jacket around it, for cooling purposes, because this bearing had such a large diameter, and because the engines could now be persuaded to rev to more than 5,500 rpm, the bearing rubbing speeds were considered so high as to need cooling assistance. The idea was very clever in principle, and was applied to other Riley six-cylinder engines from that time — the problems connected with water freezing in winter, of silt gathering in the slim passages, and of general owner neglect, were still to be learned.

Power output was not quoted, though it was claimed that with a racing body fitted the Brooklands Six was capable of 'a good deal more than 100 miles an hour'.

Behind the engine was a very familiar looking clutch bell-housing and gearbox casing (based on that of the Nine), though this car had close ratio gears, and a neat remote-control gear change lever. The torque tube transmission, too, was clearly derived from that of a normal road car.

The new car's styling was clearly done for racing, with a very low frontal area, two seats, and a long tail so entirely full of a 26-gallon fuel tank that the spare wheel was mounted vertically, in a slot in the tank, hidden under a bulge on the rear deck of the body shell itself.

The career of the Brooklands Six was short, and not very remarkable (see Chapter V), but the car itself is important for what it later inspired. After the Six of 1932 came the 1933 Tourist Trophy cars, for which project five chassis were prepared. These were similar in many ways, except that the 9-foot wheelbase of the Six had been reduced considerably, to 8 feet 1.5 inches — this being a very important dimension, for the MPH and the Sprite road cars, plus the racing TT Sprites and Racing Six two-litre models, all used the same wheelbase, and the same basic frame.

Meantime, in 1933, there came the Grebe, a Riley model which has all the exalted status of a 'unicorn' these days, for although everyone seems to know about it, no-one seems to have seen one, and the breed is well-and-truly extinct. The name of 'Grebe' has previously been applied to the series of five 1933 racing car chassis (though this is probably not

This characteristic chassis number — even the plate is diamond-shaped — is on MPH registration number BLN 39. The 44T sequence dates from October 1932.

The facia of this MPH has almost the same instrument layout as that of the Sprite *and* Imps pictured in these pages.

historically accurate), yet it is also a fact that later in the year Riley published a brochure for a competition car to be called 'Grebe'. The brochure stated that the wheelbase would be 8 feet 6 inches (not a dimension repeated on *any* other Riley two-seater of the 1930s, which leads me to suspect that it was a misprint, or merely an aberration), that the six-cylinder engine would be the 1,486 cc unit, that there would be three SU carburettors, that there would be a sports body style, and that it would all sell for £595.

Every company has its might-have beens, and I suspect the Grebe is one of them. The MPH which followed it, however, was much more serious, and by no means as mythical, or legendary.

The first point I would make about the MPH is that it carried almost the same style as that of the Imp (the centre section of the body shell *was* the same though the tail/spare wheel layouts were quite different), and that it was such a pretty car that almost everyone raved about it. As I have already explained in the previous Chapter, the Imp/MPH style was certainly developed with an eye to what was fashionable in Italy at the time — not even the most blinkered Riley enthusiast would disclaim an obvious connection with modern Alfa Romeo styling. But that was certainly nothing to be ashamed of. As MPH owner Tim Dyke wrote in the *Bulletin of the Riley Register* for March 1974:

'In my humble book, the MPH was the prettiest motor car ever built, Riley or not. The proportions of the car, from all angles, are quite perfect, and what other conforms to this criterion? The Zagato influence is there, no denying it, but even if you regard the Imp and MPH as direct plagiarism of the 1750 Alfa Romeo, did not our friends from Coventry do it better? Please observe the Alfa Romeo side on, to see what I mean; an otherwise perfectly proportioned vehicle, spoiled by that ultra-high running board.'

By 1934 it was high time that Riley once again had a good, nice-looking, two-seater sports car to sell, for the Brooklands Nine had been dropped, the Brooklands Six had not gone into production, neither had the Grebe, and the March Special had been too large, too heavy and not nearly sporting enough. As I have already made clear, the Imp was first seen in the first half of 1934, and at about the same time it was joined by the MPH. Prototypes had already been run in the RAC rally, and in the RSAC Scottish rally, so the public launch was hardly an enormous surprise to Riley enthusiasts.

Quite simply, the MPH was a lusciously-styled two-seater, looking remarkably similar to the smaller-engined Imp, though with a longer wheelbase, bonnet and front wings, and one which combined every well-proven piece of Riley engineering experience with the most beautiful modern styling. It is an abiding mystery to everyone who knew the MPH's

Below left: The MPH tail was sleek and sexy, but not quite the same as the Sprite which followed, and not at all like that of the Imp, which had an exposed spare wheel. Note the huge brakes.

Below: The driver's side of the MPH, opened up – not only to expose the engine, but also the pedal layout.

contemporaries that so very few of these cars were sold; as one lover of 1930s 'thoroughbreds' mused, recently — 'It can only have been the price'. That price, in fact, was £550.

The chassis design of the new car, no doubt at all about this, stemmed from that of the 1933 TT Six racing cars, and therefore from the general layout of the Brooklands Six of 1932. The lack of doubt, quite simply, is because the two MPH prototypes were built up on the basis of dismantled TT Six chassis — specifically those registered KV 5694 and KV 6079 — both of which had been used in the Tourist Trophy race.

The chassis, in other words, had an 8 foot 1.5-inch wheelbase, with the 3 foot 11.75-inch front and rear tracks, with the worm and full wheel steering gear, and with the characteristic leaf spring locations first seen on the 1932 Brooklands Six. The wheels were 3 x 19-inch centre lock wire-spoke types, with 5 x 19-inch tyres, and there were huge 15-inch brake drums, operated via Riley's now familiar continuous cable compensator, and adjustable layout. To improve on roadholding, and stability particularly under braking, there were torque reaction rods linking brackets on the front axle, and the front cross-member of the chassis. The steering column, incidentally, was adjustable for rake — which was one way of getting as much room as possible in a very cramped passenger compartment.

The engine, as announced, was to be available in one of two sizes; the

MPH's did not have much room in the cockpit. I guess that those famous 1934 publicity pictures featured a *very* slim model girl!

'normal' 1,633-cc unit if the owner had no interest in motor sport (and, therefore, in the $1^1/_2$-litre class limit), or 1,458-cc unit which was a size resulting from the use of a 57-mm cylinder bore. In general the detailing of the engine was familiar, for the water-cooled centre bearing was fitted, and the front engine mounting tube slotted through the crankcase from one side to the other. In addition there was a ribbed sump casting, and a Scintilla Vertex magneto was standard. Cooling was by pump, fan and thermostat. In this particular application, there were twin horizontal SU carburettors, and two beautifully sculpted three-pipe fabricated exhaust manifolds. The peak power output of the 1,458-cc engine was quoted as 'over 70 bhp', which promised sparkling acceleration by the standard of the mid 1930s.

From the autumn of 1934, in line with other 1935 models in the Riley range, the MPH was also offered with the 15/6 engine, which actually had a 1,726-cc capacity, though this was only marginally more powerful that the 1,633-cc unit.

Right from the start, too, there was to be a choice of transmissions — that of a four-speed manual gearbox (without synchromesh) with the 4.77:1 final drive, or of the Armstrong-Siddeley built 'Wilson' four-speed pre-selector transmission with a 5.0:1 final drive, In both cases, there was torque tube drive to the spiral bevel final drive, in the now-traditional Riley manner. The pre-selector gearbox might not have been the most 'sporting', but it was still nevertheless the transmission found on the majority of MPHs.

It was the styling of the MPH, however, which made the most impact, for it had the wonderfully sensuous lines already mentioned, there was a noticeable fin on the tail (nice — but entirely without function), and the rear wings which flared so rakishly were cropped off high at the rear, which allowed all the spray from the tyres to soak the car following behind!

The tail, incidentally, was smooth and looked capacious, but it housed only the spare wheel and the 15-gallon fuel tank. This, incidentally, was one important point of difference from the Imp, whose spare wheel was exposed to view. There was a small stowage compartment behind the seats, but this was usually full of hood, side-screens (if fitted) and the hood sticks. If you went touring in an MPH, you did it with very little luggage!

Detail styling features included the use of very small (5-inch diameter) Salora headlamps, to reduce wind resistance. These were supposed to be quite adequate for MPH-speeds at night. That surviving MPHs seem to use larger headlamps tells us that this was perhaps wishful thinking!

The cockpit, in truth, was very small, and not at all suitable for tall or bulky drivers, even though the seats were adjustable fore-and-aft. The combination of a wheel close to the driver's chest and a narrow cockpit made cornering a 'shuffle-the-wheel-through-the-hands' operation — perhaps that's where old-fashioned driving instructors get their ideas from, even today!

Like the Imp, already described, the MPH was on sale for little more

Just a bit of stowage space behind the seats of the MPH — the spare wheel and the fuel tank live under the sloping tail.

Below right: The MPH's six-cylinder engine was one of those power units which always looked right – the sort to gladden the eye of the enthusiast even before it is fired up.

Below: The delicately contoured exhaust pipe run of the MPH was designated to miss the chassis frame, the engine mounts, and the starter motor, and to tie up to the twin down pipes. Not easy!

than a year. Launched in May 1934, it was already a back number by the summer of 1935, and it was replaced by the four-cylinder Sprite (already described) for 1936. Sales, frankly, were very disappointing for such an exciting, and fast car— only 17 cars were built.

One prototype version, described more fully in a later chapter, was the 'MPH-ERA', which was the prototype MPH fitted with a de-tuned $1\frac{1}{2}$-litre six-cylinder supercharged ERA engine! All very exciting, and possessed of fearsome performance for a road car, but as it would probably

have cost over £1,000 (and *that* was Supercar pricing at the time) only the one car was built.

Let Tim Dyke's comment on the MPH, from the *Bulletin,* sum up the MPH's character!

'It is, in the flesh, even more beautiful than its photographs would have you believe. Its performance is nothing to write home about, adequate, without being scintillating . . . It takes an enormous time to enter, has no weather equipment you could seriously use, has luggage capacity for one and a half toothbrushes, its ride some might describe as akin to the curate's egg, and in its natural state has an uncomfortably low axle ratio for fast touring . . .

'The Sprite was still beautiful, but the corner had been turned, and sadly we had to cover that most perfect of prows with a silly birdcage to assuage the aerodynamicists . . . I have no doubt that it [the Sprite] was an excellent machine in all respects, more performance, more practicality, more of many things, but somehow the flair had gone, as was the beloved silky six.'

No other true road-going six-cylinder Riley sports car was ever put on sale, and for that reason the MPH is at once a desirable, and rather pathetic, monument to the period. If ever there was a fine engine looking for a fine chassis, the six-cylinder Riley unit was it. All the evidence shows that there was a great deal of potential still locked away inside that engine, and the pity is that Riley never developed the unit further.

I am led, inexorably, to the conclusion that they neither understood, nor cared about, the sports car market. What a waste!

Does the Triumph Dolomite of 1934 look at all like the MPH of earlier 1934? If it had been fitted with flowing front wings (which *were* planned), the resemblance might have been obvious. Donald Healey was involved in the design and development of both cars.

IV

Contemporary Reports

It was only when I sat down to collect available data on the sporting Riley covered in this book, that I realised how few of them had ever been put through the full rigours of a road test at the time. Independent tests by magazines were, in any case, by no means as numerous in those days, (more than 50 years ago), as there were few important rivals to *The Autocar* and *The Motor* in the 1920s and 1930s. Even so, compared with the number of published tests of cars like the MG and Triumph marques, the appearance of a sporting Riley test in print was a real rarity, and therefore a considerable treat for the enthusiast.

It was not that Riley was reluctant to have its latest cars tried out by the press — *The Autocar* and *The Motor* were much more influential in terms of setting standards, and offering opinions, in those days, and could certainly not be ignored — it was just that there always seemed to be more important Rileys to be handed out for test at the appropriate time. This reinforces the impression I have, too, that the Riley family was never completely committed to the design, production, and marketing of Riley sports cars, even though the company indulged in a considerable amount of motor racing, for the sake of good publicity, and engineering development, as the 1920s gave way to the 1930s.

Accordingly, while this Chapter certainly quotes the opinions of journalists about the 'sporting Riley' period spanned by the Redwingers, and the Sprites, it often cannot back up the opinions with detailed speeds and performance figures, and other statistics, from the period. In some cases, in fact, I have drawn on the reminiscences of owners published some years 'after the event' as well — some of the more illuminating memories coming from *The Autocar* and its famous 'Talking of Sports Cars' series, which did so much to sustain the enthusiast's interest during the Second World War.

The Autocar published extensive impressions of a four-seater 'All-Season' model in June 1923. Although not a pure-bred Redwinger (the name, after all, had not yet been officially coined by factory publicists), the rolling chassis, and the general road manners were identical, for here was a 9-foot wheelbase chassis'd car, with the 4-foot tracks, a 4.0:1 final drive ratio, and a smart, lightweight, body style on which the true four-seater Redwinger was certainly based.

The test car (registered MD 606) was painted blue, with contrasting (probably black?) wings. It had wire spoke wheels, but no front brakes, and a close-coupled four-seater layout for the passengers. The magazine mistakenly called it an '11.9-hp' engine, which was certainly wrong, as the capacity was the usual 1,498 cc and the price tag was £450.

All in all, it was an intriguing specification, which the testers clearly enjoyed:

'Very few motorists travel 800 miles by road well within two days and enjoy it. Very few cars run this distance comfortably and without calling for adjustment somewhere. This, however, was part of a Whitsuntide programme for the crew of a Riley four-seater sports model . . .'

The car was entered for the London–Edinburgh trial by the magazine, of which it was said that:

'. . . the car ran beautifully, the crew were made thoroughly sleepy by the even rhythm of a schedule speed on flat main roads, and the only diversion for the driver was caused by an embarrassing collection of watches . . .

'On Kirkstone pass the Riley showed its mettle, passing, with plenty in hand, five other competitors, though deliberately driven over the steepest part of the corners — a performance rendered possible almost entirely by the four speeds at the driver's disposal . . .

'We lost one spare wheel carrier nut, and we adjusted the footbrake twice. Twice we put in a little water, and, naturally, petrol and oil — of the latter very, very little. The engine is one of the finest of modern sports engines with a good healthy beat and great power . . . How the Solex manages to give that power and a consumption of over 30 mpg for fast work is difficult to determine, but it does it . . .

'Both brakes are good, and could be excelled only by four-wheel brakes, which would be admirable for so fast a car. The body is comfortable, and there is ample leg-room in front, though not so much for a long man behind . . .'

The Motor tried out a four-seater Redwinger in the Cotswolds, in the autumn of 1924, and gave it what they called a 'strenuous test'. HP 9679 clearly had much in common with The Autocar machine, but had a polished aluminium body style. It was, in fact, the self-same car which is now owned by Dr Andrews, and which is depicted in these pages.

In a two-page trial, the testers wrote more of the surroundings explored than of the car itself, but they found time to say that.

'Their way from Coventry had led them down the Old Fosse Way, where the speedometer of the Riley had stood for miles on end between 50 mph and 60 mph, as the car sped along those long, unfrequented stretches with just enough bend in them to prove its stability and easy steering . . .'

Talking of 1-in-12 hills in the Cotswolds:

'The Riley is, of course, a four-speeder and could take practically all these hills in third at about 40 mph, its maximum on this gear being about 50 mph . . .'

And on the subject of open-road motoring:

' . . . the car should be capable of averaging something like 40 mph, providing the best use is made of the centrally located change-speed lever . . .
'On the twisty lanes the Riley demonstrated its ease of steering, comfortable suspension and the excellence and softness of its brakes which, even at speed and on wet roads, enabled the car to be pulled up rapidly and progressively without locking either wheel . . .
'The design of the seats was such that they could be occupied for several hours on end without either driver or passenger feeling in the least degree tired, stiff, or sore . . .
'In the course of the run the petrol consumption was measured and found to be at the rate of 24 mpg over a distance of 120 miles, which included a good deal of hill-climbing and pottering on sodden roads . . .'

And, how right *this* was:

'The body is particularly attractive, for the combination of red wings, wire wheels, chassis and trimming contrasts pleasantly with the aluminium panelling . . .'

On the whole, one must wonder why so very few of these cars were ever built and sold.

The Brooklands Nine was an altogether more specialised machine, perhaps more 'race' than 'road' car, so it is perhaps not surprising that the magazine testers rarely got their hands on one. *The Motor* looked nostalgically at the Brooklands during the dark days of the Second World War, stating that the new car:

'. . . came on to the market in 1928, and at once captured the imagination of the enthusiast . . . Throughout the four years it was in production the Brooklands Riley Nine remained one of the hottest cars in the 1,100-cc class, both in appearance and performance . . .

'As a road car the Brooklands model was quite outstanding. It handled extremely well, with very accurate steering . . . The driver felt in full control of the car and the gear change was a delight to use . . .

'It had very real performance, with a maximum of over 70 mph in third gear and about 90 mph in top, and other qualities in keeping. The Brooklands Riley Nine is remembered as a British sports car second to none in its class.'

When reviewing the career of the Brooklands in 1978, William Boddy, the editor of *Motor Sport*, commented that:

'*Motor Sport* got a Brooklands Speed Model for road-test in 1929, and although I suspect it wasn't driven out of London, the driver was full of praise for it. It climbed Fitzjohn's Avenue [the road up from Swiss Cottage to Hampstead village] in top gear, did 70 mph in third, would cruise silently and with a complete absence of fuss at anything from 35 to 60 mph, and had a guaranteed road-speed of 80 mph . . .

'I recall how, many years later, when I was enduring a series of very used Austin 7s, friends used to try to persuade me to change to a Riley 9 — "better brakes, a proper chassis, a real engine", they said . . .'

The full-blown race cars were obviously much less civilised, as American writer Henry Manney discovered when he sampled Rodney Smith's ex-works car (VC 8304) in 1978:

'. . . linked switches for mag, and fuel pump are flipped on and the engine is started up, bringing a mellow burble, a curious twittering noise, and the rattle of many clearances. The gearbox is a beast, especially with a high bottom gear and crash pinions, and getting away from rest involves a certain amount of crunching, double declutching or not. Third and top aren't so bad as they are both close and constant mesh but the Riley wasn't made for modern stoplight driving. Furthermore "No matter what anyone says" (quoth the proud owner), "cable brakes don't work" although they did seem to produce enough retardation to get stopped in time.

'At real speed it is a bit unnerving to find the road so close to hand, and there is a fair blast of air over/around the aeroscreens . . . As far as handling is concerned, a goodly amount of understeer is present on slow, tight corners in spite of the quick steering ratio but everything is relaxed on the straight as long as the road is smooth. Bumpy sections invite sharp hops from the rear suspension . . .'

The Autocar's illustrious Sports Editor, 'Sammy' Davis, was a good deal more diplomatic when driving a road-equipped car in April 1929:

'It is very difficult to convince certain people that a car used for racing, or suitable for racing, can be an excellent machine for everyday use on the road . . . Just out of curiosity and to see whether the development encouraged by such races as the TT is actually beneficial, one of the Riley speed models used in that race last year was taken for an ordinary run.

'The car is certainly capable of 92 mph, according to the state of tune of its engine, but when taken on the road its maximum was 80 mph. The point which would at once interest the average motorist is the car's astounding performance on top gear. True, it would not run at 3 or 4 mph on that gear, but, on the other hand, it would take in its stride hills which cause the ordinary driver to use third, or even second . . .

'Further, the machine is perfectly comfortable, much more comfortable than many ordinary touring cars . . . There are no road shocks and no hardness is noticeable in the suspension . . . The really attractive quality of the machine, however, lies in its immense sense of power without noise. It will cruise at anything between 30 to 60 mph without the passengers being able to hear the exhaust, and the engine appears to be doing nothing.

'It goes without saying that the Riley holds the road. It is very doubtful if there is a car which can be taken round corners faster, and its steering is pretty near perfection. Then the gear change is fascinating, for the close ratio box allows the driver to do exactly as he wishes with the little short lever, using no force and neglecting the clutch if he feels so disposed.

'This particular car, incidentally, was fitted with the new type brakes, the previous examples having been fairly good, but not really being big enough to cope with the car's speed . . . As fitted at the time of testing, the brakes were no good at all. They had undoubted promise as far as the mechanism in the drums was concerned, but the cable operation had so much whip that no sort of control could be obtained over the brakes. Since the trial the brake actuating mechanism has been remodelled; a re-test proved that the car at last has brake mechanism worthy of it.

'It would be quite easy, for example, to arrange luggage space partly in the tail, partly by adding suitcase carriers at the side . . . The hood is already adequate, and the screen as well, while, naturally, there is no real necessity to have a screen which lies flat on the scuttle . . .'

The same magazine relies heavily on Riley reminiscences in its famous

Talking of Sports Cars series, which enlivened so many thin 1940s war-time issues. Random notes from just two of these features show how their charm has persisted, over the years.

In March 1943, *The Autocar* commented that:

'Few small cars have been more genuinely sports cars than the Brooklands Riley. In fact, in appearance and equipment and performance the production version probably came closer than was usual in such comparisons to the racing machines which performed so successfully . . . The nearest *The Autocar* got to testing one of these cars was when in 1930 "Casque" took one through the MCC London–Land's End, securing a "gold" with great dash. He wrote, at the time: "It goes up hills like a scalded cat, sliding beautifully round corners with the rear wheels shooting dirt and stones, and with that magnificent feeling of irresistible power." '

Later in the feature, an owner, Urban Burrows, wrote that:

'Speed, cornering and roadholding are up to usual Riley standards, and no words of mine are necessary to convey just how high those standards are. Braking, until minor adjustments in equalisation were carried out, was a little hectic . . . It is with some trepidation that I approach the subject of maximum speeds. I will go no farther than to say that 80 mph, 55 and 40, can be exceeded on top, third and second respectively, without undue fuss or bother . . .'

In 1941 Norman Routledge had written, of his own Brooklands Nine:

'As for performance, I got 84 mph in favourable conditions and nearly 70 on third; on second gear about 52 was the limit, and nearly 37 on bottom . . .

'It was quite lively, and superb on corners, but the brakes!'

There was, it seems, complete unanimity about the car's main characteristics — and if the brakes were really as bad as all that it is a miracle that so many have survived into the 1980s!

The Imp, on the other hand, was a much more normal road-going sports car with less temperament — though the Riley factory was still not willing to let it out to the magazines to make performance figures. No doubt the rather limited power/weight ratio, and the rather 'gentle' performance which resulted from this, was the reason for this.

Perhaps it was a rather sweet little car, beautifully styled, but not otherwise outstanding, for pundits often seemed to dismiss it while waxing lyrical about other Rileys — Rivers Fletcher, for instance, in *Thoroughbred*

& Classic Cars, merely stating that he 'always liked the Imp best with a plain gearbox instead of the usual preselector box' — and left it at that!

I turn, therefore, with gratitude to 'Talking of Sports Cars' once again, and find that the Imp featured twice — with two cars being discussed in 1943, and a further example in 1944.

H. S. Linfield, prefacing the owners' views, wrote that: 'With Rileys I always feel on particularly safe ground — that is, in the knowledge that a large section of the sports car populace is interested in this make . . . — in which case I have again to wonder why so few of the various models were therefore sold when they were new!'

Linfield himself went on to write that: 'Myself, I have always been attracted by the lines and general layout of the Imp two-seater, along with the six-cylinder model that I regard as having been a companion model, the MPH two-seater. Neither was produced in large numbers, and I have often wondered why more was not made of them by Rileys from the production point of view.'

C.E. Piggott, who owned a 1935 model (registered ADU 801) then wrote that he bought his car in 1937, when it was in a truly awful condition, rebuilt it and converted it from pre-selector to manual transmission, and that he believed 'that the Imp was largely experimental, and I have rarely found two alike in certain details . . .' The car, in good condition, could achieve about 75 mph, and he recorded 28 mpg overall. He also recorded that he reconstructed the hood and its frame, to give him eight inches extra width and four inches extra head room. In addition: 'this car apparently never had side curtains.'

Herbert Euston's car, described in the same feature, was a 1935 model, which had been bought third-hand, with 13,000 miles on the clock:

'It was a sheer delight to drive, and had all the characteristics of a real thoroughbred . . . In its standard form, I do not believe that the car would rank as the fastest of its type, but this is entirely due to the body and chassis being heavy and extremely robust in construction . . .

'The absolute maximum speed in standard form under favourable conditions would be about 73 to 75 mph, and I doubt if the latter figure could be exceeded without efforts being made to reduce weight.

'The acceleration of my car did not appear to be particularly rapid, in spite of the quick gear change, but this may have been a result of the fact that my experience of light sports cars has been limited to specially-prepared super sports Morgans (three-wheeler) . . .

'The only serious criticism I can make is that the upholstery is not particularly comfortable; this is due to the back-rest having no springs and very little padding . . . Also the hood is not of sufficient width to cover the cockpit completely, which results in the driver's arm and leg receiving large quantities of rain. No arrangement has been made for carrying the smallest attache case . . .'

Even if all this smacks of praising with faint damns, there was no doubt
that the Imp had great charm, as W. S. Gibson, a one-armed driver who
owned AKV 443 as a new car from 1935, confirmed:

'I think that the Imp might be considered as a transitionary type
between the vintage and modern sports car, having vintage aspirations
in its road holding, hard springing, high-geared steering, visibility
and exposure-to-the-elements qualities, and linking up with the
moderns through such features as the preselector gearbox and
centralised chassis lubrication . . .'

(This car's attraction to Mr Gibson was that the pre-selector controls
suited his disability — for he had lost his right arm.)

'In standard catalogue form the Imp had the ordinary twin-
carburettor 9-hp engine . . . I do not think it was quite equal to dealing
with the inordinate drag imposed by the preselector box . . . I had the
crankshaft come in half in the first few thousand miles, which was not
the result of over-revving. It was replaced by the works; the second
crank went after the engine had been modified, and this failure was in
part caused by the engine period which ensued from the rebuild and, I
must admit, was also probably the result of a 'blind', during which the
engine was run practically flat-out for some 100 miles.
    'The performance figures in this [standard] form were a nominal
71.4 mph at 4,500 rpm, with which the reasonably accurate
speedometer agreed, and some 55 mph on third at the same revs. I
have no data for acceleration figures, but the getaway was quite good
without being sensational as compared with that of other cars on the
road.
    'The brake drums were of considerable size and the brakes
themselves very good when properly adjusted, but decidedly tricky if
this precaution was overlooked.
    'Of the pre-selector gearbox I can only say that it was a fitment of
which I took a very poor view, though fully appreciating its qualities
for those who like such things. I am convinced that it was this which
effectively killed any chance of getting real performance except by
drastic and expensive modifications.
    'The body was very well made, but heavier than it might have
been and this criticism could more or less be applied to the whole
car . . .'

— after which rather lukewarm account, which nevertheless ended with the
conclusion that: 'I developed a good deal of affection over the 65,000 miles
we covered together', I feel that I ought to turn to a much more exciting
sporting Riley — the MPH.

Here, once again, was a fast and beautifully-styled Riley sports car that few people bought, and which was never dignified by a full-scale test analysis from one or other of the weekly magazines. In their initial technical analysis, *The Autocar* suggested that 'the design of this model is a determined effort on the part of the men responsible, to produce a car of literally outstanding road behaviour, a car with a capacity for an honest 85 mph, and yet to be as smooth, as flexible, and as quiet as any costly super saloon.

'In due course a Road Test will be carried out [it never was] but in the meantime it may be mentioned that the MPH Six is said to compass from 6 to 85 mph on top gear, and that it has averaged 70 mph from place to place without vicious driving.'

Michael Bowler, then of *Motor,* but later the founder/editor of *Thoroughbred & Classis Cars,* drove Bob Lutz's MPH in 1972/73, and reported on it in a feature accompanied by stunning photographs. Michael opened his comments with the sentence: 'Surely one of the best-looking cars of all time was the Riley MPH' — and no-one is seriously arguing with those sentiments. At the same time, the car had undergone 2,500 hours of restoration at Tula Engineering, in Hertfordshire so perhaps he was wise to write that:

'The whole car is beautifully finished and I hardly dared take it out on the open road . . . Getting in required a certain knack of knowing which knee to put in when and where, but once in it was quite comfortable with the wheel close enough for the effort required.

'The clutch is set to engage at 500 rpm, so the tickover is about 400 rpm and the engine is scarcely audible. First and second on the wide ratio box were fairly noisy — the usual preselector howl — but third and top were quiet; with a little help from the accelerator changes were pretty jerk-free both up and down.

' . . . with gearing around 20 mph per 1,000 rpm it should be capable of all-day cruising at 75 mph, with a maximum around 85-90 mph. And comfortably too; it rode well with marginal scuttle shake but no rattles. Roadholding was typical of the era; direct steering and no noticeable roll gives good cornering on good surfaces, with the amount of rubber on the road as the limiting factor; bumpy corners are taken slightly Christopher Robin fashion — hoppity-hop — although the solid weight of the car limits this.'

That famous MPH one-off — KV 6079, fitted with a de-tuned 1½-litre ERA engine — was described in 'Talking of Sports Cars' in September 1941 by Rivers Fletcher, who was much involved with its concept, when new. However, in the introduction, H. S. Linfield makes yet more trenchant comment about the limited sale of Riley's 1930s sports cars:

'Another thought brought up, one thing always leading to another in these matters, is why the MPH Riley and the Nine Imp, too, were not more widely sold. Riley performance, for size of engine, and general excellence of design are proverbial; they are cars with engines you can cane without ill-effects; their makers have always given them brakes and roadholding of exactly the kind for sports cars. Add to all this the fact that these two-seater models had precisely the right sporting appearance and one would have imagined that they would have been best sellers among sports cars.

'Their inner manufacturing history I do not profess to know, but perhaps for various reasons Riley's never wanted to make them in appreciable numbers. It is not usually in cars of this type that a manufacturer who also sells in more popular markets is able to make money; and — I am not thinking of Rileys in particular — owners of such cars, meaning ourselves, are often an expensive nuisance to the manufacturer! . . .'

Which is an interesting comment on a subject already discussed in other chapters. Meantime, Rivers Fletcher added his own comments about the behaviour of the MPH-ERA prototype, the single car produced in 1935:

'This particular ERA engine was somewhat de-tuned to enable it to function satisfactorily on pump fuel, but even so, the performance turned out to be pretty colossal — well over 100 mph at 6,500 rpm, which was by no means the rev limit of the engine. The chassis was found to be entirely adequate for the extra urge, very powerful brakes operating through 15-inch drums, light, high-geared steering, and a strong and light racing-type chassis all being part of the standard specification.

'On the road, as might be expected, the car's outstanding feature proved to be its terrific acceleration — a little too much loud pedal and it would spin its wheels with the utmost ease, even on top gear. The weight distribution seemed just about right, and thus the car retained the good cornering qualities for which Rileys have for so long been noted . . .'

This car needed the radiator repositioned, about six inches further forward, to accommodate the ERA engine's supercharger, which rather destroyed the MPH's good looks. The ideal solution was to fit a longer wheelbase chassis, and Rivers Fletcher later recalled that ERA were offered a 'one off experimental frame' for this purpose. Although everyone got very excited about the prospects, and drawings were made, such a conversion was never completed. The MPH was returned to standard, and sent back to Coventry.

The MPH-ERA would, of course, have been monumentally expensive, and I doubt if more than a handful would have been sold. By this time, in any case, Rileys had lost interest in the MPH, for they had the easier-to-build, cheaper, and almost as rapid Sprite at the development stage.

Riley enthusiasts must have been quite amazed to see *The Autocar* actually publish a full road test of the Sprite, in the summer of 1937, for by this time they must have thought Riley was always going to hide away its sports car products in catalogues and price lists. The car used in this test was registered CRW 910 (which was one of a whole series of CRW . . . numbers taken out by Riley, in Coventry, at the time), was fitted with the characteristic 'waterfall' grille, and like most other Sprites, it had the pre-selector transmission.

The Autocar test team, headed by H. S. Linfield, seemed to like the car very much, headlining their test report: 'A Proper Little Sports Car of High Efficiency, Which is Practical for Everyday Use.' In the course of the test, with figures taken at the Brooklands race track, they recorded a mean maximum speed of 83.33 mph with the screen folded flat, and a mean top speed of 80.18 mph with the screen raised to its normal 'road' position, with 0–30 mph, 50 mph, 60 mph and 70 mph in 5.4, 13.1, 18.8 and 29.7 seconds respectively.

By the standards of the day, therefore, the Sprite was a quick car, let down only by its fuel consumption, recorded at 'approximately' 21 to 22 mpg over a distance of 500 miles. Some of this thirst, no doubt, could be attributed to the hard driving given to it by the testers, and some by its considerable weight, which was accurately measured at 2,211 lb.

A car's worth, of course, is not merely measured by the statistics, so it was interesting to see that the testers thought that:

' . . . there does really seem to be a connection between the extremely fast 1½-litre cars which have performed so strikingly in the Tourist Trophy race, and this sports version offered in the ordinary way to the enthusiastic buyers . . . This Sprite is not a racing car, but in part of its behaviour it shows that it is a close relative . . . Few cars put into the hands of the public, sports type included, give a stranger an identical impression of being so much of a sound piece of engineering work . . . it is stable to the extent of being almost impossible to overturn, although cornered much faster than is general practice; it has the acceleration that will take it through gaps in traffic . . . 'An absence of frills is appreciated; everything fitted has a purpose, and rightly belongs to a sports car . . . 'In its whole appearance, the ohv engine breathes efficiency and purpose, by its neat arrangement and clean finish . . .'

The testers, as usual, veiled their true feelings behind elegant phraseology, but there is no doubt that they found the suspension hard, the steering heavy at low speeds, the pre-selector transmission rather unsuitable to the rest of the package, and the driving compartment distinctly cramped. But then, wouldn't the 1980s Sprite enthusiast also admit to the same problems, if he was being honest with himself?

Naturally, the Sprite also featured in *The Autocar's* 'Talking of Sports Cars' series in October 1942, and the interesting wrinkle to this story is that its original owner was a dashing young man named Maurice A. Smith. Not only was Maurice Smith the son of the magazine's influential managing editor, G. Geoffrey Smith, but he later became editor of the magazine himself, from 1955 to 1968.

In the introduction, H. S. Linfield wrote that:

'I look back upon the experience of that machine with the greatest pleasure. It is true that one had to find a place for one's feet and legs, as space was somewhat cramped beneath the steering column and in the pedal area, but once you had fitted yourself to the car it was most comfortable and undoubtedly a "real" small modern sports car.'

[The author, who is somewhat taller, and broader, than the dapper Linfield ever was, sympathises. He found it quite impossible to drive Ian Hall's magnificent black Sprite, and had to plan carefully his entry or exit into the driver's seat!]

'With that exceptional ability of Rileys to rev freely and smoothly, the engine would go round to an indicated 5,500, in fact, and the red mark on the rev counter was set at that figure . . . Positive high-geared steering ($1\frac{3}{4}$ turns lock-to-lock), 15-gallon tank, fine brakes, and stability of just the right kind combined to make up a car that one coveted, and that showed clearly the benefits to be gained from racing experience.'

By the time the review was written, the car (originally registered CHP 109, and similar to the actual road test car of 1937), had long since changed hands, had been badly damaged in an accident in California, and had been bought by an American enthusiast, Robert O. Cox, and painstakingly restored. This particular part of the story, indeed, is more of a tribute to the rugged virtues of the Sprite's construction than to the new owner's opinions, as the car had done very little running since it had been rebuilt.

And that, as far as the sporting Riley, and contemporary reports, is concerned, was that. The Sprite was the last of the *real* sporting Rileys, for after the Second World War, the company's policy had changed considerably.

As recently as 1982, however, Mike McCarthy, *Classic & Sportscar's* Editor-at-Large, drove a nicely-maintained Sprite (DJJ 678, fitted with the 'traditional', rather than the 'waterfall' radiator grille). His driving impressions noted that:

> The engine is naturally very torquey, thanks to its very long stroke, pulling from very low revs indeed. When you do start using the revs the low murmur from the exhaust behind you builds up into a most satisfying growl, overlaid with a trace of gear whine, and the car moves off very briskly indeed.
>
> 'You do know, however, that you're in a car that's over 40 years old when it comes to the brakes, steering and suspension. To slow the car requires a hefty push on the brake pedal, but that is the only complaint: the brakes are progressive and effective and pull the car up four-square. The large steering wheel, close to your chest, requires considerable muscle too at parking speeds, but soon shows that it is light and direct when you've built up some speed. However, it does jiggle around in your hands, and eventually you realise that it is better to let the car effectively find its own course, keeping steering corrections to a minimum. Surprisingly, although bumps can be felt at the wheel, they don't seem to deflect the car from the straight and narrow.
>
> 'The ride can best be described as lumpy rather than harsh, the car almost dancing along on rougher surfaces but without knocking your teeth out like some other cars of the period. This characteristic is emphasised by considerable scuttle shake and a rather floppy feeling from the bodywork.'

Finally, he admitted that:

> 'I must confess, never having driven a pre-War Riley before, I often wondered why — apart from their looks — there was such a mystique about them. I should have realised, from the numbers still driven enthusiastically by members of the VSCC at race meetings, sprints and such like, that a considerable amount of their charm comes not only from what they do as the way they do it. They are an enthusiast's car *par excellence:* consider me now a paid-up member of the Riley Fan Club.'

Doesn't that tell you everything you need to know about a sporting Riley?

V
The Racing Rileys

One day, I am sure, a complete book will be written about Rileys in racing. It is a fascinating story mainly involving cars with Nine, six-cylinder, and $1\frac{1}{2}$-litre 12/4 engines, some with superchargers and some unblown, some with bodies recognisably developed from cars sold to the public, others looking very special indeed. In this book I can only hope to summarise the careers of the various families.

I should say, right away, that I believe there to be quite a bit of controversy over the identity of some cars — Riley, like many other manufacturers, before and since, were not at all reluctant to swap registration numbers from car to car if the events of the moment suited them — so I quote registration numbers only with some trepidation.

As to the naming of some cars (what was a Grebe and what was not, what was a racing MPH, and what was a TT Sprite, for instance?), I have tried to follow the agreed definitions, rather than try to be clever and inventive.

The great days of the Riley in racing covered the period 1927 to 1937, when the factory's 'works' team was actively involved, and when diligent young development engineers like Eddie Maher (who later did a similar job for the BMC competitions department at Abingdon) squeezed the best out of the twin high-cam, hemispherical-head engines.

From 1932, however, the factory's tuning achievements were often matched, and sometimes beaten, by the efforts of ace mechanic/tuning specialists like Freddie Dixon, and Hector Dobbs — Dixon being a gritty north countryman from Middlesborough, and Dobbs being a motor trader from the south.

We must not forget, either, that the Riley six-cylinder engine also formed the basis for the famous ERA single-seater racing power units, though by the time these were completely developed there was very little actual Riley hardware left in evidence. The ERA era, if you'll pardon the pun, is described in more detail in a later chapter.

From 1922 to 1927, Riley's competitions effort was really concentrated on Victor Wallsgrove, the Redwingers, and the racing versions of the side-valve cars which he developed, or encouraged. The Redwinger, however, was much too closely based on the design of the side-valve touring cars, and was seen at its best in the long-distance trials of the period — Exeter, Lands End and Edinburgh being *the* most famous. It was after a particularly outstanding performance in the 'Edinburgh' of 1925, after all, that Rileys not only out-numbered other competing makes, but took an astonishing number of Gold awards, and where the Riley Motor Club was founded.

Nevertheless, Victor Gillow built a racing version of the side-valve car in 1924, and won two races at Brooklands — the Whitsun Light Car handicap at 77.5 mph where he started as 'limit' man in the usual handicap race, running without wings, and (according to *The Autocar*) 'soon drew away, and settled down to a fine gait', and the Long Handicap (over the 'long' distance of 81 miles!) at the August Bank Holiday meeting, where his car averaged 81.5 mph and narrowly beat eight other competitors. His second place in an earlier race had so surprised the handicappers that they penalised him seven seconds before he even started the winning race! That average speed, incidentally, was more than 10 mph better than the claimed *maximum* speed for a standard two-seater Redwinger . . .

Thereafter, as with most successful Brooklands-based racing cars, Victor Gillow's car fought a battle as much with the circuit's completely incorruptible handicapper, 'Ebby' Ebblewhite, as he did against other cars, though he used the machine until 1930. By 1927, in fact, the car had reached the limit of its performance, and was soundly beaten by Reid Railton driving the prototype Nine, in that car's very first race! Later in the day, however, this was avenged, when Gillow's car averaged no less than

The start of the 1931 Ulster TT, with three Brooklands Nines in evidence at Ards. No. 29 was Gillow's car, No. 30 Cyril Whitcroft, and No. 31 Chris Staniland — Staniland finishing fifth and winning the class.

89.43 mph, and lapped at 93.44 mph, to win the Gold Plate — some going for a side-valve Riley! After the car rolled at Brooklands, at high speed, following a tyre burst in a close finish, it was time to retire the plucky old machine, and let the Brooklands Nine take over.

There was also the sand racing saga, begun by Wallsgrove beating Raymond Mays's 'Brescia' Bugatti at Skegness in 1923, and then going on to produce a short-chassis Redwinger with skimpy oyster-shell wings, which was campaigned successfully in 1924 and subsequent seasons, not only on sand, but in hillclimbs and speed trials. In its ultimate condition, this slim little car was reputed to be capable of 106 mph, though its current owner, Redwinger expert Richard Odell, has seen no more than 95 mph while racing the car at Silverstone.

The advent of the Riley Nine ultimately changed everything — not only the production car scene at the factories, but for Riley in competitions. During 1927, Riley supplied a Nine to Parry Thomas's company, Thomas Inventions Development Co. Ltd., to develop a sports car from the basic chassis, and this eventually caused Victor Wallsgrove to resign his post, and set up in the motor trade in Coventry. From 1927 to 1932, when the first of the six-cylinder race cars appeared, the Brooklands Nine, and its developments notched up success after success for Riley, sometimes as 'works' machines, and sometimes as privately-entered machines.

The prototype itself, still with the high over-rear-axle chassis, was entered at the 1927 Autumn BARC meeting at Brooklands where, driven by Reid Railton, it won the '90 Short Handicap' at 91.37 mph, but set a fastest lap of no less than 98.62 mph. Writing in his monumental 'History of Brooklands Motor Course', William Boddy commented that:

'The Riley Nine was a most classic car . . . It was the forerunner of the famous Brooklands sports-model . . .'

— while *The Autocar's* race reporter commented that:

'In the second race, a 90 mph Short, the new racing Riley Nine developed outstanding speed in the hands of R. A. Railton, its sponsor, and without apparent effort, ran right away to win at 91.37 mph, by nearly half a lap, thereby causing immense consternation among those present who had entered 1,100-cc cars in the 200 Mile race and had never even thought of the Riley.'

It is worth breaking off here, however, and recalling the remarks of an earlier Brooklands personality, talking about the longevity of certain racing engines:

'A quarter-mile sprint is one thing, but a full half-mile is a *very* long way indeed.'

The Ards circuit, in the Tourist Trophy of 1932, with George Eyston's Brooklands Nine at the hairpin, and Whitcroft's car right behind him. They finished second and first overall, respectively.

Even if he was not entirely serious (though some Brooklands-based cars were notoriously reluctant to work properly for more than a few seconds at a time!), the quote serves to emphasise the difference between instant performance, and long-distance durability. The 200 Miles race competitors need not have worried, for the prototype racing Nine did not appear again on the track in 1927.

Early in 1928, George Duller (who also drove big Bentleys with success) took out the prototype Brooklands Nine on the track after which it was named, setting new Class G International records up to 10 miles, and up to 97.85 mph; in the autumn, incidentally, H.W. Purdy added to the sprint records with another 'endurance' tuned Brooklands (this one entered officially by Victor Riley, but prepared by Thomson & Taylor), up to 500 miles and 87.09 mph.

The first 'team' entry in long-distance motor racing came in May 1928, when three new Brooklands models (one of which was driven by *The Autocar's* famous sports editor 'Sammy' Davis, who had won the 1927 Le Mans race in a 3-litre Bentley) started the Essex MC' Brooklands Six Hour race. Thomson and Taylor had prepared the cars at Brooklands (this company actually making the first few 'production' Brooklands models, in any case), with Reid Railton and Ken Taylor in charge. This race was for road-equipped sports cars, which meant that a hood and windscreen had to be fitted — the hood having to be raised for the first ten laps.

In this, the first-ever real race for the Brooklands, there was good news and bad. The disappointments were that two cars retired — one with a deranged gearbox, and one with a broken oil feed pipe on the crankshaft. The wonderful news was that K. S. Peacock's Riley won its class, and finished an excellent fourth place overall, on handicap behind Ramponi's Alfa Romeo, Dingle's Austin Seven, and Sir Henry 'Tim' Birkin's $4^1/_2$-litre Bentley.

Later in the year, five Brooklands started the Tourist Trophy race on the Ards circuit, one of them being the Maclure brothers in a factory-prepared car. As with most British events at this time, it was a handicap event, which resulted in Clive Gallop's T & T car actually leading the event at one point, but several crashes due to driver error thinned the ranks, and once again it was Peacock's car which won its class at 56.98 mph; the outright Winner, Kaye Don in a Lea-Francis 'Hyper' averaged 64.06 mph. The Brooklands was already beginning to demonstrate that you did not need a large engine to produce a fast car — just an efficient one.

In the next few years the list of Brooklands successes got longer and longer, as more and more cars were delivered, and more was learned about the tuning potential of the splendid little engine. The Brooklands, in fact, always handled well, and was always remarkably fast. Its brakes let it down from time to time ('Sammy' Davis commented as much on this, in later years), and the two-bearing crankshaft had to work very hard to stay in one piece when revved extremely hard, and subjected to considerable power-tuning.

In the four big long-distance British events of 1929, a Brooklands Nine was well placed. At Brooklands the very first Junior Car Club 'Double Twelve' event (12 racing hours on Saturday, a night locked away in *parc ferme*, and 12 more racing hours on the Sunday) saw a Brooklands

The start of the Brooklands Riley's finest hour in 1932 — the Tourist Trophy race, which Cyril Whitcroft (No. 17) won outright from George Eyston (No. 16). Other Brooklands were driven by Chris Staniland (No. 18), A. von der Becke (No. 19), Freddie Dixon (No. 20), Tommy Wisdom (No. 21), and Victor Gillow (No. 22).

take sixth place, and second in class behind a twin-cam Salmson. In the Irish Grand Prix, held at Dublin in July, there were no fewer than eight Rileys entered for the $1\frac{1}{2}$-litre race held on the first day, and the result saw George Eyston's car take fourth place (beaten only by one Alfa Romeo and two Lea Francis sports cars, all with larger engines), with Victor Gillows' car sixth, Jack Dunfee's car seventh and Cyril Whitcroft's car eighth.

In the Tourist Trophy race at Ards, the illustrious team of drivers included 'Sammy' Davis, John Cobb, and the Hon. Brian Lewis (all in 'works', as opposed to T & T cars, for the centre of gravity of Brooklands Nine racing had moved to Coventry by this time), and the result included a class win for Davis, who also finished 12th overall. The fourth of the long-distance events was the 500 mile race — that end-of-season Brooklands thrash held on the outer circuit, where an engine blow-up could leisurely be repaired over the long winter months which were to follow! The best finish was by Martin and Stapleford in eighth place, at 80.12 mph (a $4\frac{1}{2}$-litre Bentley won at 107.32 mph), which was also good enough for a class win.

In 1930 the record was even more creditable, and this time a Brooklands achieved an outright win in a major race, albeit on handicap. In the spring, no fewer than 59 cars started the second 'Double Twelve' race at Brooklands, and by the end of the first day the best of the Brooklands, driven by Cyril Whitcroft, was handily placed in fourth, behind two big Speed Six Bentleys and an Aston Martin. On the second day, Whitcroft (partnered by Hugh Hamilton) moved up to finish third overall, behind the two Bentleys, averaging 69.96 mph in spite of rain slowing all the cars near the end.

That was splendid, and so was the eighth overall (and first in class) by a privately-entered Brooklands, driven by R. T. Horton in the Tourist Trophy race at Ards, but the best result of all was reserved for the Irish International TT, at Pheonix Park, Dublin. The first day's race, for $1\frac{1}{2}$-litre sports cars, attracted a big entry — 28 cars — of which 19 were supercharged, but of which five were Rileys. Victor Gillow's car, the only Riley to finish, and one of only four un-supercharged cars to cross the line, won the race outright on handicap — and was also fourth fastest on scratch times, too. The race took 3 hours, 36 minutes and his average speed at Phoenix Park was no less than 72.2 mph. Gillow's car was running with cycle-type wings (though others in the race had the more normal 'road-car' swept wings), and the driver himself was on some sort of personal high for reports described him as 'wild' and 'lurid' — there was one reference to his car 'leaping over kerbs and down banks as he roared past other cars with the agility of a mountain goat. It was amazing that the car stood some of the shocks it must have received . . .'

After that there was really no way that the Brooklands cars could do even better in 1931 — nor did they — but there were still many splendid

This MPH model (registered KV 9763 — a factory number — and driven by Jack Hobbs) was used in the 1935 Monte Carlo rally, but the wintry conditions beat a gallant effort.

results in the long-distance races. (In the space I have, here, I cannot even mention the short-distance and sprint successes, nor the trials and rallies in which the cars performed so creditably!) It was still a good year — Rileys took their class in the Double Twelve, Irish Grand Prix, in the Tourist Trophy race, and in the Brooklands BRDC 500 miles race.

In the TT race there were five Brooklands Nines, four of them being 'works' cars officially entered by Victor Riley, the fifth being A. F. Ashby's own car. In the race, Gillow crashed — overshooting Quarry Corner and rolling the car — but the other three 'works' cars finished, that of Chris Staniland taking fifth place overall at a record class average speed (on VC 9204), the others being second and third in class, behind him.

The 500 Miles race, held at the beginning of October, and run under handicap, as usual, was the usual carefree thrash, with the 1,100-cc cars being asked to *average* 95.78 mph, to keep up with the big Bentleys, which were set 113.19 mph!

Unfortunately the fastest Rileys were not the ones which finished — half way through the race Cyril Whitcroft's car not only led the event outright, on handicap, but had averaged 104 mph, while Land Speed

This MPH, hood and screen down, but aero-screens erect, took part in the RAC Rally of 1936. Wasn't it beautiful?

record holder Malcolm Campbell's works car had been lapping at 110 mph in the practice sessions. On the 'hare-and-tortoise' system, however, all three 'works' team cars retired with the same clutch problem (perhaps the power was becoming too much for the transmission?), and a privately-entered Brooklands, driven by Miller and Eggar, took fourth place overall at 92.83 mph. Make no mistake about this achievement, however — that was still a higher average speed, over 500 miles, than Reid Railton's prototype had averaged in a sprint race four years earlier.

The Brookland's most magnificent racing year, however, came in 1932 when Brooklands cars won the Junior Car Club's 1000 Miles race at Brooklands outright, the Tourist Trophy race outright and achieved a second overall in the BRDC's Brooklands 500 Miles race. It wasn't quite a clean sweep, but it was near enough! The most amazing aspect of all this competitions success is that Rileys were neither ready, nor seemingly able, to back up competition results with the marketing of a good high-performance road-going sports car; the Brooklands was now quite obsolete as a catalogue car, and the Imp was still two years away.

The 1000 Miles race was the rather shorter successor to the Double Twelve, but cars still ran on two days, and were locked for the night in between, so that no work could be carried out on them. It was in this race that the Brooklands Six first appeared (I describe this car later in the chapter), along with five Brooklands Nines. Although it was difficult for the average spectator to follow the complex handicapping of this race — especially as the cars did not start *en masse* — the cognoscenti soon realised that the Brooklands Nines were leading the entire event. At the end of the first day, it was Sutton and Harvey who led, but even more creditably it was two ladies (Elsie 'Bill' Wisdom and Joan Richmond) who were in second place.

On the second day, the men soon retired, while leading, and thereafter nothing could stop the ladies who, driving VC 9204 (Stanilands' 1931 Tourist Trophy car, by the way) went on to win the event at an average speed of 8.41 mph; they had taken 12 hours 23 minutes, 53 seconds to achieve this result, and only narrowly beat off a Talbot challenge. The Whitcroft/Maclure car finished fifth, but in the hubbub of a great 'Ladies' Day' that achievement was almost ignored.

Then came the equally meritorious outright win, on handicap, in the Ards Tourist Trophy race, at which the Brooklands had performed so well, for several years. On this occasion, in August 1932, no fewer than seven Brooklands Nines were entered, of which four were entered by Victor Riley, one by Mrs. Wisdom (though she did not drive — her husband Tommy, and Sammy Newsome of Coventry shared that pleasure), one by Victor Gillow, and a seventh by that abrasive character, Freddie Dixon. It was, in other words, a significant event in more ways than one.

Dixon was starting his first-ever race in a Brooklands Riley, though he already had an amazingly successful career behind him on motor cycles, and now he was turning his hand to racing cars. Not only was he a fast and fearless driver, but he was an extremely meticulous preparer/mechanic of any machine. His TT race car was an 'ex-works' Brooklands (VC 8303) which had been raced by Victor Gillow, and which he had taken back to Middlesborough, stripped out, studied, and rebuilt to his own exacting standards. By the time he had finished it was lighter, had more precise

In the RAC Rally of 1935, which finished up at Eastbourne, the weather was clement enough for this Imp to run hood-down much of the way. BPLI — now *there's* a valuable number today!

steering, better brakes, had a special body style, and more power than the 'works' cars.

Unfortunately, having practiced very rapidly, he had needed an engine gasket change on the night before the race, spent much of that night rebuilding his car, and subsequently admitted that his race-day crash was due to fatigue! Before then, however. he led his Riley Brooklands rivals — notably Cyril Whitcroft and George Eyston — for 20 laps. The story goes that he was then distracted, and confused, by a pit signal, arrived at Quarry Corner much too fast, and then proceeded to crash the car *over* the hedge into a field, sometimes described as containing cabbage, sometimes rhubarb! Well-known archive pictures show Dixon still finding time to switch off the engine ignition — in mid-air — before it could over-rev itself in the ensuing melee!

Following this Whitcroft, who had never been far behind the flying Dixon, took over the lead, and crossed the line a minute and a half ahead of George Eyston's sister car. The winning car was registered VC 8304, and averaged 74.23 mph over a race distance of 369 miles.

It was the first time this historic sports car race had ever been won by a 1,100-cc class machine. In its editorial comment column the following week, *The Autocar* commented:

'It is a pleasure to record the victory of the 9 hp Riley in the Tourist Trophy after a race as hard fought as any that can be remembered. Mr. Victor Riley deserves the success in every sense of the phrase, for he has upheld the British colours for many years. Congratulations are due to all concerned in the production of the cars, and to Commander Whitcroft and G. E. T. Eyston, their drivers . . .

'One has only to compare the speeds class by class with those recorded four years ago, and, even making allowances for the fact that this year the road was dry throughout the race and that the cars carried less equipment, it is obvious that development has vastly improved performance generally.'

[Whitcroft's finishing speed, in fact, was 2 mph better than that set by Caracciola's vast, supercharged, Mercedes-Benz sports car in the 1929 TT race!]

After such a stupendous showing, a Brooklands would have had to win the end-of-term 500 Miles race outright to make a similar impact — but in the event it could only finish second, fourth and fifth! Interest had been raised by Freddie Dixon producing his Riley-based 'Red Mongrel' single-seater, and entering it for this, its first event (and driving it all the way from Middlesborough to Brooklands prior to the event!), but the 'works' Brooklands Nines were also strongly fancied.

Dixon's car soon broke down with a variety of mechanical derangements, as did Ashby's very special privately-developed car, while

Whitcroft's car broke a fuel pipe. After three-and-a-half hours George Eyston's off-set single-seater MG was in the lead (this was a handicap race), but Cyril Paul's Brooklands lay fourth and was *averaging* 100 mph round the outer circuit!

Much of the heart went out of the race following Clive Dunfee's fatal accident in a big Bentley, but the Rileys battled on. At the end of the day one of the deadly rivals — Horton's MG Midget, a 750-cc car — won the day, but Brooklands Rileys took second (Cyril Paul), fourth and fifth place. Cyril Paul's car averaged 99.51 mph for five whole hours.

Even though the factory was now turning its attention to the faster and more exciting six-cylinder cars, there was still time for the Brooklands Nine to add to its laurels. In 1933, not only did the cars put up excellent performances at the Tourist Trophy race (where W. R. Baird, driving one of Victor Gillow's cars, finished sixth overall — beating all the six-cylinder Rileys! — while Dixon's car was placed fourth, but later disqualified), but there was outstanding new success in the Mannin Beg, and Le Mans 24 Hour races.

Mannin Beg and Mannin Moar were two new 'round-the-houses' races promoted at Douglas, in the Isle of Man, and although these were picturesque events they were soon to die from lack of interest. In 1933 the Mannin Beg race (for cars up to 1,500 cc without superchargers, or for smaller-engined supercharged cars) was not only won outright by a Brooklands Nine, but it provided the first-ever Riley victory for Freddie Dixon. Raymond Mays and Humphrey Cook (already working hard on the 'White Riley' project, described in the chapter concerning ERAs) were entered in six-cylinder cars, but did not appear.

Dixon's much-modified Brooklands, set fastest practice lap on the four-and-three-quarter mile circuit, and lay fourth at an early stage in the

One of the well-known team of TT Sprites — this one being AVC 20, driven by A. von der Becke, at Shelsey Walsh in 1935. The result was FTD for 1,500 cc sports cars.

230 mile race, visited the pits to deal with a seized universal joint, clawed his way back up the field remorselessly, and finally took the lead after 36 laps. Thereafter, nothing could touch him, and he beat Mansell's supercharged MG Midget by 15 *minutes* after every other car, supercharged or not, had retired.

At Le Mans, in June, two cars — KV 5392 and VC 8304, both familiar 'works' Brooklands cars — started the 24 Hour race, the first car having French drivers, the second being driven by K. S. Peacock and competitions manager A. W. von der Becke. The French car eventually retired with engine problems, but the two Brits kept going in spite of minor chassis problems, to take fourth place overall, at 66.83 mph, behind three 2.3-litre eight-cylinder supercharged Alfa Romeos. Not only that, but the Riley won the class, the handicap category, and beat the 1,100-cc record by 9 mph! Could anything more have been asked of the Riley?

Maybe not, but in 1934 the factory went back to Le Mans, not only with their one remaining 'works' Brooklands (KV 5392 — all the others having been sold off), but a trio of race-modified Imps, and two of the six-cylinder machines. With only four hours to go, the Brooklands, once

TT Sprites undergoing final preparation before the 1935 Le Mans race. The cars had 1¹/₂-litre engines, and the best finisher was the Von der Becke/Richardson car, which took fourth place.

again driven by Peacock and von der Becke and aiming for the Biennial Cup (awarded for the best aggregate performance over two consecutive years — a crafty French ploy to ensure continuity of entries), lay fourth behind two of the six-cylinder Rileys and a 2.3-litre Alfa Romeo, but by the end they had slipped back one place. This was still good enough to win the Biennial Cup, and the 1,100 cc class. No wonder that Riley's advertising described the marque as: 'The most consistently successful car in the World'.

By this time the 'works' team *and* Freddie Dixon were completely bound up in the development of the six-cylinder racing cars, so there was only time for a mild flirtation with a potential successor to the Brooklands, which was the Ulster Imp. The Imp, in any case, had some racing ancestry in its chassis design, for this was a shortened version of the MPH's layout, and that was a refinement of the first six-cylinder chassis which dated from 1932.

Three modified Imps had been entered at Le Mans in 1934, where all had finished behind the successful Biennial Cup-winning Brooklands Nine, but a team of four cars known as Ulster Imps were prepared for the 1934 Tourist Trophy race. These had special bodies, without doors, which were not as low as the Brooklands had been, and had the shorter, 7ft 6in., wheelbase of the Imp road car, and race-tune engines. In spite of being wrongly geared for the TT race (the regulations which applied that year were very restricting, so standard road-car ratios had to be used), all four cars finished, with honour, the best (von der Becke's machine) winning its class and taking ninth place. The Ulster Imp, however, was never an important car in the team's strategy.

The six-cylinder race car saga began in 1932 with the launch of the long, low, and rangy Brooklands Six, which I have already described in an earlier chapter. Not only did this car have the new chassis frame, underslung at the rear (and different in every detail from that of the Brooklands Nine which had served Rileys so well), and the 1,486-cc six-cylinder engine, but its vast fuel tank meant that the spare wheel had to be mounted vertically, in the extreme tail, slotted into a recess at the back of the tank, and having to be hidden under an unsightly hump in the bodywork. A less honest management would no doubt have claimed all manner of subtle aerodynamic advantages in such a body style!

The first race car, driven by George Eyston, appeared at the 1000 Miles Race in May 1932 (where it was quite overshadowed by the magnificent 'Ladies' Day' victory of the Brooklands Nine), but made no impact at all on the event — even Boddy's Brooklands circuit history ignores it.

Later in the year, however, Eyston took another Brooklands Six (registered KV 1862, with very non-Riley looking bodywork) to Montlhery to attack International Class F endurance records. Eyston, called 'le Recordman' by the French, was almost a season-ticketholder at the French

No, its not an ERA — this is Raymond Mays driving the White Riley at the Brooklands Whitsun meeting of 1934.

track, and along with Edgar Maclure set a number of new records, at up to 200 miles, and up to 111.65 mph. Early in 1934 he revisited Montlhery, again with Maclure, to add Class F records up to no less than 2,000 kilometres at 102.35 mph.

Later in 1934, the streamlined car made another appearance, at Brooklands in the 500 Miles race, where its shape and specification was ideal for outer-circuit racing. Alex von der Becke drove the car, and eventually finished second overall at 101.65 mph — behind the Riley 'Dixon Special' with Dixon himself at the wheel.

The original car (now registered KV 1861) was entered in the 1932 TT race for Edgar Maclure to drive, and once again it was overshadowed by the victorious Brooklands Nines. Maclure, however, finished eighth overall, and won his class — a class, incidentally, which included Alvis, Frazer Nash, Lea Francis and Aston Martin opposition.

That, however, was the end of the Brooklands Six's short racing career, for it was not to be used again by the works. Instead, for the 1933 Tourist Trophy, a team of four new six-cylinder cars, called Grebes by some Riley historians, or TT Sixes by others, were prepared. Compared with the Brooklands Six, these cars had considerably shorter wheelbases (8 feet 1.5 inches compared with 9 feet), and had a re-arranged fuel tank/spare wheel arrangement, so that the wheel was positioned across the tail rather than in line with the chassis, leaning forward on to a more box shaped tank. The overall length, too, was much reduced. The engine and transmission was much as before, but there were 15-inch instead of 13-inch drum brakes. These cars were registered KV 5694, KV 5695, KV 6078 and KV 6079. Drivers were George Eyston, Cyril Whitcroft, Chris Staniland and Edgar Maclure.

In the race itself, there were signs of hurried pre-event building and preparation, but the 1932 winner, Whitcroft, managed to struggle through, to finish eighth, and win the 1,500-cc class — this being exactly the same achievement as the Brooklands Six had achieved in 1932!

Once again, however, this was a short-lived breed of racing Riley. Of the seven chassis laid down in 1933, two were eventually re-designed and re-built as prototype MPH road cars, one went to Raymond Mays and Peter Berthon (this one was never used as a Riley race car before it appeared, late in 1933, as the 'White Riley', the forerunner of the ERA single-seater), while three were acquired by Freddie Dixon to become the basis of his famous 'Dixon Specials'.

At this point, I ought to try to differentiate between the 'works' six-cylinder cars (MPHs in 1934, and TT Sprites thereafter), and the Dixon Specials. Although Dixon received a great deal of help from the factory, his Specials were very much his own development projects, running with distinctively low, long-tailed, racing bodywork, without wings, while the TT Sprites were the genuine 'works' cars. There seems to be no doubt that Dixon's engines were significantly more powerful than those produced by the factory, for 'Our Freddie' was very secretive about what went on inside his engines, of which there were several different sizes, and specifications — depending on the rules and conditions applying to each race entered.

A pair of new so-called Racing MPH six-cylinder 'team' cars were prepared for the 1934 Le Mans 24 Hours race (KV 9477 and KV 9478 — a third car, registered KV 9763, was also built, but did not race at Le Mans). I say 'so-called', because these cars were really up-dated versions of the 1933 six-cylinder race-car chassis, fitted with body styles rather like those of the Ulster Imps. The important difference, however, was that they were the very first Riley race cars to use the pre-selector transmissions.

One of the famous Dobbs offset single-seater Riley race cars, which used a Sprite-based chassis. This car had a 2-litre engine, and six Amal carburettors, Dixon-style (though Dobbs always prepared his own engines).

The Le Mans outing of 1934 was a real triumph for Riley, whose six-cylinder cars kept going, and going, and going — after 24 gruelling hours it was a 'blown' eight-cylinder 2.3-litre Alfa Romeo which won, but the unsupercharged 1½-litre Rileys took second and third places, driven by Senilleau/Delaroche, and Freddie Dixon/Cyril Paul, respectively. The second placed car averaged 70.00 mph, which compared with the 74.74 mph achieved by the winning Alfa Romeo, which was at least twice as powerful. At last, here was proof that the six-cylinder engine could be as successful, and long-lasting, as the legendary and well-loved Brooklands. In the next few years this was to be proved again and again.

For 1935, Riley then built a series of six new race cars, which became known as the TT Sprites. These were not all six-cylinder engined, for this was the well known AVC 15/16/17/18/19/20 series, some of which had six-cylinder engines, and some of which had race-modified 12/4 1½-litre units. Not only that, but some had engine type changes during their careers! All nevertheless, used the same basic chassis design as the 1934 cars, which is to say that they had an 8 foot 1.5-inch wheelbase and 3 foot 11.75-inch tracks, like the MPH road cars, and the same 19-inch centre-lock wire wheels, but they were fitted with the Girling rod braking layout used on the later Sprite road cars, together with 13-inch diameter drums. All six chassis had elongated engine mountings so that either engine type could be fitted without further modification.

An excellent and detailed survey, written by a TT Sprite owner, C. F. Readey, in 1969, for the *Bulletin of the Riley Register* tells us so much about these cars, and confirms that the Riley 'works' racing effort was now very serious indeed. Merely to summarise — more than one set of manual gearbox ratios were used, from time to time, there was a whole range of straight-cut final drive gears (the 'shortest' being no less than 6.75 : 1), centre lock wire wheels could vary from 19 inches diameter down to 16 inches diameter, and it is also confirmed that 'all cars were fitted with various engines to suit particular needs, and it seems most likely that all the AVC cars had 12/4 and six-cylinder engines in them at odd times.'

A team of 1½-litre 12/4-engined cars was entered for the Le Mans 24 Hours in 1935, and put up another fine show, though by comparison with the 1934 result it had to be considered a disappointment. One car crashed, and a second caught fire, but von der Becke/Richardson finished fourth overall (behind a 4½-litre Lagonda, a big Alfa Romeo and a 1½-litre Aston Martin).

It was in the Tourist Trophy race, held in September 1935, that the TT Sprite really caused a stir (and, incidentally, literally earned its name). Four cars were entered — three officially by Victor Riley and a single example by Freddie Dixon, though all four were from the same 'AVC' batch. This was a race in which Dixon was not merely interested in winning his class, but in annihilating the handicap and winning outright as well.

This was the race in which the entire team of special racing Singers broke their steering and crashed, but it was also the race in which Dixon outpaced his rivals *and* his team mates, to win outright at 76.9 mph — this being the second fastest average ever recorded at Ards, and the fastest ever average by an unsupercharged car.

The TT Sprites were certainly good-looking (they had elongated tails, rather like those of the Dixon Specials, and were as low as possible), and they gradually took on more and more power. The 12/4 engines had little more than 75 bhp at first when running on normal petrol, but (where the regulations allowed it) were eventually persuaded to give 105 bhp by utilising an 11.0:1 compression ratio, and running on special fuel.

Egged on by the example, and the plans, of ERA, the six-cylinder engine's capacity was pushed out, eventually to reach a full 2-litre size. Not only were the 1½-litre units already available (these dated from 1932, and the Brooklands Six), with gear driven oil pumps instead of plunger pumps as used earlier, but it also proved possible to get 1,808 cc by retaining the same crankshaft and stroke, but boring out the bores to 63.5 mm.

A full 2-litre engine size could also be gained by using the large cylinder bore, and an entirely new crankshaft featuring 104.5 mm stroke; these were virtually the same dimensions as used in the 2-litre ERA engine. On petrol a full 2-litre 'six' was good for about 100 bhp, but when using methanol and a very high state of tune, up to 130 bhp was sometimes seen. That sounds fairly puny today, but was considered extremely creditable at the time.

From 1936 onwards, Riley also produced an off-set single-seater racing car, which I will describe below, but in June 1936 they also found

Kay Petre, the second owner of the White Riley, sprinting along the sea-front in the Brighton Speed Trials. Incidentally, it was no longer white by this time, in 1935!

Hector Dobbs (off-set single-seater Riley) at the Brooklands International Trophy meeting of 1936. ERAs (with Riley-based engines!) were first and second, but the 2-litre Dobbs car took third place.

time to enter $1\frac{1}{2}$-litre engined TT Sprites in the French Grand Prix at Montlhery — an event run for sports cars on that occasion, to make sure that a German car could not win it! Two of these cars were 'old' AVCs — AVC 15 and AVC 19, but the third car was new, and registered BWK 324.

It was a race in which there was no question of the Rileys fighting for the lead, as they had to face up to monstrously powerful streamlined Bugattis and the like — nevertheless they dominated their class

Barrie Gillies uses the attractive-looking Treen Special in racing events in the mid-1980s. That is a six-cylinder engine up front . . .

. . . which now has a six-SU carburettor installation, strongly reminiscent of the Dixon engines of the 1930s.

throughout, the Trevoux/Maclure car (AVC 15) being the fastest TT Sprite of all.

Later in the year, at the Tourist Trophy race, no fewer than six $1\frac{1}{2}$-litre engined Rileys started the race, against formidable opposition, and once again it was the irrepressible Freddie Dixon (with Charlie Dodson also driving the car to give Dixon relief) who won the race outright, beating four other 'works' built cars, lapping at 80.48 mph, and averaging 78.01 mph, which upped his 1935 achievement by a further 1.1 mph.

This, unfortunately, was to be the last of the TT races to be promoted at Ards, as Jack Chambers, driving his own old Brooklands Nine, crashed into a crowd of spectators, killing eight of them. As the Ulster Vintage Car Club's book about the Ards races comments:

'. . . the tragedy was too much for the local authorities to accept, and the TT had to find another circuit in future years.'

Riley's 'works' motor racing career was now coming to a close, and in 1937 the two most important successes were gained at Donington Park. In the 12 Hour Sports Car race held in July, TT Sprites were used, stripped of their lights and wings (as allowed by the regulations), but as the race started at 7 am on a Saturday, the attendance was very small indeed! Right from the start the cars jumped into a lead in their class, outpacing even the 2-litre cars by half distance, and at the finish Cyril Paul/Charles Brackenbury beat the Bob Gerard/A. D. Bateman sister car, averaged 56.56 mph, finishing second overall, just 13 miles (in twelve hours, don't forget) behind the $3\frac{1}{2}$-litre Delahaye of 'B. Bira' and Hector Dobbs.

Later in the year, the Tourist Trophy race was held at Donington, this being the first time the historic race had actually been held on the English mainland. It attracted the largest crowd ever seen, to that point, at Donington Park, and saw 22 cars, including a quartet of TT Sprites, take the start.

The pace was hot, as was the magnificent weather, and the race was dominated by the big sports-racing Darracqs. 'B. Bira', driving one of the steadily-improving 2-litre Frazer Nash-BMW 328s was also faster than the TT Sprites, which were beginning to struggle against more modern, more streamlined, competitors by this stage in their careers.

In the end the Darracqs won comfortably, only two of the TT Sprites finished, with Arthur Dobson's car (AVC 17) finishing seventh and winning its class, and Bob Gerard's car (AVC 20) ninth. *The Autocar's* race report was interesting, for it said that:

> 'Dobson, Gerard and Gee, with the Rileys, were having to stop frequently, partly for water, partly because the brakes would not stand the stress in spite of their new-type linings, all of which was disappointing for a marque which has upheld the British colours in the TT so well.'

Even 'Sammy' Davis (for it was certainly he who wrote the report) was beginning to *expect* outright victory from the Riley team, which was a sure sign that the company had reached the stage of diminishing returns from its programme which had always, after all, used production-based machines to go motor racing.

Also in July 1937, Arthur Dobson's TT Sprite won the 1¹/₂-litre race at the French GP meeting at Montlhery, with three special-bodied Rileys finishing behind him.

The Dixon Specials, and the Racing 2-litre

By the mid-1930s, there was so much racing Riley activity going on, inside *and* outside the 'works' team, that it is simply not practical, in a book of this length, to do more than mention the important events.

The Tourist Trophy had been re-located at Donington Park by 1937, and here are two of the four TT Sprites which took part. The best finish was by Arthur Dobson, in seventh place overall, with a class win. Bob Gerard is in Car. 20 — he finished ninth.

With the factory itself in mind, I should first of all mention the very special racing 2-litre model which was unveiled in 1936. This was the first, and only, pre-war 'works' racing Riley to be fitted with independent front suspension, also the first and only to be designed as a pure racing, as opposed to sports racing, car.

Riley, of course, were not about to throw away a lot of hard-earned racing experience when designing a new chassis, so the new car retained the 'bare bones' of the 8 foot 1.5 inch wheelbase TT Sprite frame, and the usual type of torque tube transmission, while grafting onto it the new-fangled Andre-Girling independent front suspension, which featured coil springs, and a somewhat complex lower wishbone linkage.

The engine in the car, as first shown, was a $1\frac{1}{2}$-litre 12/4 unit, in full-race four-Amal carburettor tune, backed by the usual type of TT

This cockpit shot of one of the Dixon Specials shows the special hand-throttle controls Dixon contrived to help him with gear changing.

Sprite gearbox, but it was also stated that the 2-litre six-cylinder engine could also be used, and there was the familiar engine mounting arrangement on the frame to ensure this.

The car was not quite narrow enough to be called a single-seater, especially as the driver's seat was still on the right, but there was an auxiliary fuel tank, and no actual seat, on the left, nor would there have been the width for a passenger to be carried. The body style was quite unlike that of any previous Riley, for it was rounded rather than angular, and had a 'fencer's mask' type of front grille; there was a long streamlined headrest behind the driver's head and seat.

Von der Becke gave the car its debut, with the 2-litre six-cylinder engine, in the British Empire Trophy race at Donington, in April, where it blew its engine, but Charles Brackenbury did better a few weeks later, in the International Trophy race at Brooklands, where he notched up sixth place. However, as far as I can gather, this intriguing car gained no further British successes.

The Freddie Dixon era, and all the escapades which Dixon himself carried out, really deserve a book on their own, for the sturdy little North Yorkshireman was really a Jekyll and Hyde character. As an ace-mechanic, engine tuner, and general preparer of racing cars, he was quite peerless, but although he could be polite and straightforward at times, he was also a very abrasive character whose two main failings were an active dislike of authority (whether that meant race-day officials, or policemen on the public highway!), and a great liking for alcoholic refreshment!

If, however, one can ignore the personality side of things, the Dixon period of racing with Rileys was still enthralling. Apart from the 'Red Mongrel', and the modified Brooklands models which he used for the first couple of his years with Riley cars, there were at least two (some people suggest three) Riley-based Dixon Specials, all of which used six-cylinder engines, in various sizes, and always with meticulously-prepared razor-edge engine tune. Dixon's secret was to consider a straight six as merely a series of single cylinder engines linked together, so he arranged for there to be one Amal carburettor to each cylinder, and set up that instrument independently of the others. Patience, and yet more patience, was needed to get the best out of a Dixon-prepared engine, which is why the cars rarely seemed to go as well when they were sold off.

The first two Dixon Specials were based on TT Six chassis sold off after the Tourist Trophy race of 1933, and they were soon re-prepared to have 1,808-cc engines, and that long, low, and singularly purposeful-looking 'one-and-a-half' seater bodywork, without wings, which would become so very familar in the years to come. Both cars sometimes appeared in the same race, Dixon lending (or — more likely — hiring) the other to well-known drivers.

In their first outing, the round-the-house Mannin Moar race at Douglas, Isle of Man in 1934 for pure racing cars, Dixon's own car retired with engine trouble, but Cyril Paul finished third in the other car. The cars were then speedily re-engined with 1.5-litre engine units to make them qualify for the Mannin Beg event (which also allowed 1.1-litre cars with

Freddie Dixon, with one of his Dixon Specials, on the way to second place in the 1936 Isle of Man Mannin Beg race, behind Pat Fairfield's 1.1-litre ERA.

Lady Mary Grosvenor in the RAC rally of 1939 (which finished at Brighton), in a Sprite modified with Brooklands wings.

supercharging) — yet again Dixon's own car had to retire, when leading, but Cyril Paul took sixth place.

Success came in minor events during the year, but the first big victory came in the BRDC's flat-out 500 Mile race at Brooklands, in the autumn. If the weather had been fine, a big car, probably John Cobb's massive Napier-Railton, would have won, but in the rainy conditions, it was Dixon's Riley-based Special which came through, to win at 104.8 mph, in a single-handed drive taking him just less than five bumpy, hours.

From this point, the Dixon success story could get lengthy (but never boring!) if everything was listed, so only the highlights can be mentioned.

In 1935, a 1,500-cc engined Special finished second in the Mannin Beg race, behind Pat Fairfield's 1.1-litre supercharged ERA. In the International Trophy race, a few weeks later, he finished second behind a supercharged Alfa Romeo. In mid-summer, by which time he had produced his first 2-litre engines, Dixon won the British Empire Trophy race, with his other 1.8-litre car, driven by Cyril Paul, third. In the BRDC 500 Miles race, of October, his car lapped the concrete outer circuit at 130 mph, but suffered tyre troubles, dropped back, but was still a member of the winning team; it was in that race that a TT Sprite, with a 2-litre six-cylinder engine, turned into a 'pure racing car' by the fitment of a

Sprite-like nose, and the removal of the wings, finished second to the Napier-Railton at an average speed of no less than 112.49 mph; Von der Becke and Edgar Maclure were the drivers.

Dixon and Paul both retired from the 1936 International Trophy race, but in the Brooklands 500 Miles race, much later in the season, Dixon and Charlie Martin shared a two-litre engined Dixon Special to win outright, at no less than 116.86 mph. That made it two wins in three outings, against cars which must have been two, or even three times, as powerful. This victory, like all the others mentioned, was achieved with an unsupercharged car, for the late John Bolster, one of Dixon's greatest friends, once told me that Dixon disapproved of this way of boosting an engine's performance for many years, though by the time *The Autocar* interviewed him in November 1936 he was beginning experiments with this process.

That, however, was the end of the meteoric Dixon's racing career for, as John Bolster wrote, many years later, Dixon fell foul of the Middlesborough police on a drunk-driving charge, lost his driving licence, and to make matters worse he then committed a similar offence while still disqualified. That made a prison sentence inevitable, and it also meant that he could never race again.

There were, of course, other well-developed, and successful racing Rileys, not sponsored by the factory, but certainly a real credit to the Riley name. Among the fastest were the off-set single-seater Specials engineered

Ian Hall pushing his well-known black Sprite through a tight corner on a hill-climb course. That's about as much roll as you ever get from a hard-sprung sports car like this.

and driven by Hector Dobbs (his six-cylinder engines, incidentally, look as though they were provided by Dixon, and that may well have been the case at first, but he later carried out his own engine tuning and preparation), the Ashby 'flat-iron' Special, and the Appleton Special.

This last, incidentally, used a cut-and-shut Maserati chassis, and a supercharged Brooklands Nine engine fitted with one of Ashby's bronze cylinder heads. Eventually, after several years' development, this engine produced 120 bhp, thanks to a Zoller supercharger (ERA used these 'blowers' by that time, and their fame was spreading), and had a single-seater body style. In that guise the car took the Brooklands Class G (1,100 cc) Mountain Circuit lap record, at 76.10 mph.

Then, in 1937, he asked for, and got from Rileys, a *three*-bearing crankcase, had a special crankshaft designed, and built by Laystall, and produced an engine that was finally boosted to no less than 183 bhp at 7,400 rpm, with the ability to exceed 9,000 rpm in the gears! All this, mark you, with unmodified, long stroke, bore and stroke dimensions . . .

In all this time, incidentally, the 'works' Rileys never used supercharged engines in an important event — which is surprising, considering that ERA, whose engine was evolved (a long way evolved, of course) from that of the six-cylinder Riley, never used anything else. One reason, of course, is that British sports car racing regulations banned the use of supercharged engines from 1934, but there was still many events, in many countries, where such engines would have been useable.

And if the various Riley engines could achieve so much in normally aspirated form, what majestic performances might have resulted from blown versions?

Remember, too, that in the 1930s, success in British motor racing was usually down to the use of great engines, for the roadholding of most cars was very similar, drum brakes were always marginal, and the performance of the tyres was nothing to get excited about. The sporting Rileys won so much because their engines were better, and more tuneable, than any others — a wonderful epitaph for the 'PR' cylinder head, and the rugged engineering which went with it.

VI
Riley Restoration

Normally, a book in this series would deal with restoration in two ways —
firstly by describing the good and not-so-good choice of cars available, and
secondly by going on to describe the wide choice of rebuilding services
available. In general, many more cars than book readers are around.

But not in this case. I have already made it clear that the choice of
sporting Riley models was wide enough, but that the numbers were always
strictly limited. I must now make it clear that very few restorers spend all
their time on Riley work, let alone on the refurbishing of the sporting cars.

Anyone going out to buy a sporting Riley should know that at any one
time he will probably have very little choice. At one extreme, if he was
looking for an MPH he would have to join a substantial queue of 'classic'
fanatics, all of whom have the same idea. At the other, he may have to
snatch the first genuine Imp or Sprite which comes on to the market, and
worry about the price, and restoration, afterwards.

Nowadays, of course, there is the question of replicas — and whereas
most owners of such machines will cheerfully admit that their cars are not
originals, there may be others seeking to make a killing by offering a
magnificently 'restored' Riley which is nothing of the kind. One day, no
doubt, one of the last, long-lost, MPH cars will 're-appear', and be put on
sale at a horrifying price; not everyone will be able to work out the genuine
vintage, or otherwise, of the chassis and its running gear.

One problem, of course, was that the sporting cars used so many
modified touring car components, and this, allied to the fact that the
genuine Riley company's pre-1934 chassis records have disappeared,
makes it so easy (if not cheap) for a valuable 'missing' car to be re-created.
One can even get replica chassis frames, ostensibly for the building of new
Riley 'Specials'.

Another is that so many of the genuine sporting Rileys either had body
modifications made to them during the 1940s and 1950s (when the concept
of a 'classic car' was unknown, and when almost any non-vintage pre-war
machine was treated with disdain), or had their bodies crumble away
almost completely due to general rot and neglect. The result was that in the

This is the sort of Aladdin's Cave that any Riley restorer would give a lot to own. Can you identify the four-cylinder engine on the floor?

1960s and 1970s quite a number of genuine sporting Rileys needed completely re-created bodies before they could once again go on the road, to be enjoyed. If, therefore, you were to come across a Riley that you suspected *might* only be a replica, you could probably draw no obvious conclusions from the state, and equipment, of the body shell.

Both the important British Riley clubs — the Riley Register and the Riley Motor Club — look on restoration and maintenance as the most important aspect of their activities, and they have built up a network of resident experts on the various models, and ranges. Each club, and each expert, also has his own specialist suppliers. One way or another, the restoration of a between-wars Riley is never likely to be defeated for lack of expertise, or for lack of knowledge.

In preparing this chapter, and in checking out other sections of this book, I was fortunate to be able to talk to two of the most prominent Riley restorers in the business — Barrie Gillies, of Bradfield, near Reading, whose stock is a real Aladdin's Cave for Riley enthusiasts, and Ian Gladstone, of Blue Diamond Services, in Langport, Somerset. In both cases, I came away with a deep sense of inferiority, not only of my own failings as a mechanic and re-builder of cars, but of the number of years it would take me to amass the knowledge they already have!

I should start, straight away, by considering the problem of body restoration for *all* Rileys, not merely the sporting cars. Remember two facts — that the last true 'Coventry Riley' was built getting on for fifty years ago (most of the cars have now passed their half-century), and that the Luftwaffe did a very good demolition job on much of Coventry during the Second World War.

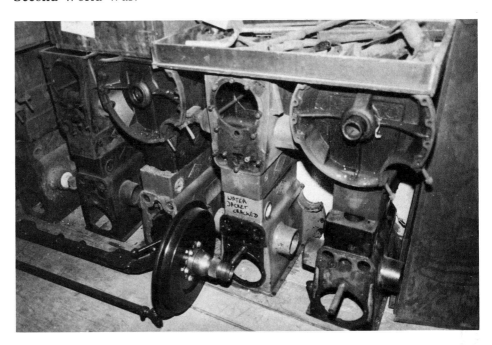

Cylinder blocks for six-cylinder models are now scarce, but there is ample supply of small four-cylinder Nine blocks. This is just one corner of Ian Gladstone's workshops at Langport.

This meant that no spare panels, sections, or even jigs, survived into the post-war Nuffield-Riley, and BMC-Riley period. Even in 1945, it seems, owners of pre-war Rileys were on their own. Worse still, no drawings (if drawings ever existed of body panels — nothing will convince me that the panels of something as rare as an MPH were actually drawn up; these would merely be beaten out, by hand, over wooden formers) have survived, either of panels, or of the wooden frames on to which these skin panels were fixed.

Officers of both the important clubs confirmed that they were powerless to help members over major new body items. All they can do is to put a member, in need of information, in touch with another member who has the same model of Riley, so that the second car's body may be studied.

This does not mean, of course, that bodies cannot be re-constructed. Many a Riley owner has done his own re-building over the years, while the professional Riley specialists take the wrecked or disintegrating cars, which they have been commissioned to restore, to competent body makers with the concise instruction: 'Copy That'.

As far as all the sporting Rileys are concerned, their bodies took shape around a wooden skeleton (the material was always ash which has a very straight grain, and which can also be 'persuaded' to take up other shapes without distintegrating), to which simply contrived skin or bulkhead

Below left: Obvious reminder — be sure to count the teeth on crown wheels and pinions before snapping up a new item. There were various different ratios on the sporting Rileys.

Below: An engine doesn't have to be exactly right to be useful as a basis for parts for another model. Much of this $1\frac{1}{2}$-litre engine could be used to help re-fettle a Sprite, for instance.

panelling was later attached. Those with general knowledge of 1920's and 1930's assembly techniques find nothing in the layout of a Riley to surprise them, for the whole shell of a sporting version came apart like a massive constructional kit, once the appropriate bolts, stays, and clips were removed; compared with this, there was very little welding of large panel to large panel.

It would be a very brave (and possibly foolish) restorer, incidentally, who assumed that such basically hand-built bodies were symmetrical, and that anything could be assumed to be paired! Barrie Gillies tells the story of restoring his ex-works rally car, ADU 28, a Gamecock Six, sending off its rear wings to be re-made, and finding that the new panels were not at all the same as each other:

'I protested, but the supplier merely said, "You asked us to make wings like these, and we did!" They had, too, the originals were up to an inch different in certain respects.'

Gillies also told me that he once discussed the whole question of Riley bodywork, wings in particular, with the well-known Riley dealer, and racing driver, Hector Dobbs. If Dobbs ever had an awkward customer whose car had been in an accident, and who wanted a matched pair of wings, they would actually go up to the factory, from Hampshire, and select the nearest possible match from wings hanging up in the stores:

'It was no good asking the factory to send a *pair* — they would merely send you the first left-hand, and the first right-hand, wing they could unhook from stock.'

In the Riley scheme of things, one body builder would spend all his time in one section of the factory using wheeling machines and a simple former to produce panels, while another man, using another wheeling machine (and probably left-handed instead of right-handed!), would produce the same panel for the other side of the car . . .

Gillies, in fact, actually moved into the Riley restoration business, having been an enthusiast for many years, when he began to think about structural panel supply. Then, as now, the supply of basic sheet metal panels, or sections, for old cars is simply not done 'for stock', and Gillies's first thoughts were to build floor pans for the Lynx:

'I had three or four people looking for the 12/4 Lynx floor pan, which is made of steel, and actually sits on the chassis, on rubber pads, then the wood is built up on that floor pan, and the panelling on to that frame.

'So I lined up to make about six of these floor pans, came over and talked to this farmer [near Bradfield], went out and bought myself a

bender, a folder, and a guillotine — and at that time somebody ran into the back of my wife's Monaco!

'So I hawked that around a number of restorers, but no-one wanted to touch it, for the steel floor pan was damaged in the back, the woodwork was damaged, the panel work was damaged, and they didn't like touching Riley saloons. Once you start in on the woodwork you never know where you're going to finish.

'In the end the insurance company paid up for a write off, and let me keep the wreck. So I started to do it up myself.'

It is likely, incidentally, that a few original body sections, or wings, are still lying around in some Riley enthusiast's garage or storeroom (though never on a dealer's premises), for there has been quite a vogue in recent years for the building of racing specials which has released standard panels for re-use. Such machines inevitably begin to look like TT Sprites, or Dixon Specials, with new and skimpy coachwork. It pays to advertise, they say; no matter how hopeless it may seem, some restorers have struck pay-dirt by actually asking if any spare bits of this or that are still around!

At the end of the day, though, sporting Riley body restoration usually has to be done 'to pattern' — by copying another car — or by re-creating the crumbling remains of what has survived. That this can be done is proved by the variety of half-completed bodies in one of the large buildings used by Barrie Gillies for his restorations. Barrie has had complete body frames done by specialists like Nick Jarvis, of Ascot, who is not only an expert in that particular field, but is also a Riley enthusiast who owns one of the surviving TT Sprites, and a 'Dixon' 2-litre racing Riley.

When a body shell is to be restored, the question of re-creating the original, or of modifying it to an individual's needs, has to be settled, and the case of Nick Jarvis's TT Sprite is a perfect example. The TT Sprites,

Above: The Armstrong-Siddeley pre-selector gearbox is extremely complex, internally, but there is no problem in getting them restored, and new parts are available.

Above left: The Armstrong-Siddeley-built pre-selector gearbox (as opposed to the ENV-built pre-selector) was a popular Riley fitting in several larger-engined models. Such transmissions were fitted to the MPH and Sprite sports cars too.

The complicated parentage of the pre-selector transmission fitted to Riley sports cars is clear from this plate riveted to the side of the casing.

1¹/₂-litre engines, for Sprites, are generally very reliable, and there is plenty of cooling water around the cylinder bores.

like the Imps and MPHs of the period, had very restricted cockpit space, and were clearly built around small drivers in the Dixon mould. To make the car even driveable for himself, Nick produced a modified style, with the steering column raised, and the pedals re-positioned, merely so that he could change gear without his leg coming firmly into contact with the steering wheel.

In re-building any sporting Riley, only a hidebound purist would complain if the car was given non-standard seats, or a modified driving position, to make it possible for it to be driven at all. One Riley enthusiast I consulted in preparing this book suggested that there were two reasons Rileys used pretty girls in their Imp and MPH publicity pictures — one was to attract magazine editors, and the other was that no normal-sized man could have got into the car and remained comfortable! He also said that:

'The MPH and the Imp are very impractical motor cars for anyone taller than 5 foot 6 inches.'

It was no good fitting the side curtains to a mid-1930s sporting Riley, they say, if you wanted to be able to drive it (there would then be no place for the right arm and elbow), but on the other hand you had to fit the side-curtains in poor weather or get thoroughly soaked . . . It was a Catch 22 situation, and most enthusiasts, then and now, settled for wearing weather proof clothing, *and* getting wet. As to warmth, and a lack of draughts — don't be facetious, no-one expected a British sports car of the period to be spacious, civilised, or comfortable; I have a friend with probably the best SS100 in the world who confirms that he has never fitted the side curtains on his car (which resembles an MPH or a Sprite in general layout), because he doubts if he could turn the steering wheel with them in place.

Most of the cars covered in this book have very cramped cockpits, not only in width, but in terms of general driving space, elbow-room (literally) and pedal reach. If you are prepared to settle for something not quite as overtly sporting as the two-seaters, then a March Special, or a Lynx, is much more comfortable.

Riley experts also confirm that there is no need to over-restore Riley bodywork to impress the experts, and that some 1950s and 1960s re-building projects went way over the top. The expert panel beaters who might shape metal for a restoration should also be told about this — there is not much *economic* point in having wings and bonnet panels produced to Rolls-Royce standards if the car they are to adorn is a middle-class Riley. This also applies to trim materials, too, for there is no point in taking Rolls-Royce periods of time (and using the same quality of seat re-construction, and leather facings) to rebuild a car which cost £300 or £400 in the 1930s.

When it comes to the mechanical rebuilding of a sporting Riley, the problem is one of time, money, and patience, rather than of being able to find certain components. Whereas, on the one hand, six-cylinder blocks in good condition are rare, pre-selector gearbox cases are so plentiful that Barrie Gillies's mechanics use them freely as a substitute for axle stands! Before long it is likely that there will be more modern replica TT Sprites than surviving 'real ones', while some parts are so freely available that an acknowledged expert like Ian Gladstone suggests that 'there will be no shortages in my lifetime'.

In general, there is a good supply of Riley hardware available — old stuff restored, new off-the-shelf items to original patterns, or re-manufactured material — which is probably a good thing as thousands of 'real' Rileys are still in existence, and regularly used by their owners.

When I started preparing this book I was astonished to hear that there

All the chassis frames for Riley sports cars are simple in layout — this is the bare bones of a Sprite, the design being very similar to that of the MPH, and also related to the Imp too.

One of the Riley 'trade marks' is the use of torque tube transmission from gearbox to final drive. This adds to overall vehicle weight, but provides excellent rear suspension geometry and location. Note the 'No oil' sticker on the differential cover!

may be well over 7,000 pre-war Rileys still in existence — and this means Rileys running, or being actively re-built, not merely identified as heaps at the bottom of a pile in a breaker's yard. And, as Barrie Gillies quipped: 'You only need 10 per cent of those being worked on at any one time, and there's plenty of business for any restorer who is interested.'

The two major Riley clubs are trying as hard as they can to keep all pre-war Rileys on the road, not only by holding, and re-manufacturing, stocks of 'consumable' mechancial parts, but by sometimes taking a deep breath and arranging for important items like crown wheel and pinion sets for back axles to be machined once again.

The Riley Register claims to have a good supply of original factory drawings for most mechanical items, though these are dispersed all around the country, and are by no means freely available to all restorers; some have never even been allowed to look at them. One of them told me that he was not sure of the provenance of some drawings, and was happier to have new parts made to pattern, using existing (but old) Riley components as his originals, and taking advice on the best engineering material to be used in each case.

But where does the original 1920s and 1930s material come from. In the case of the side-valve cars, it appears only rarely, and is seized upon with glee — Richard Odell, who is *the* Riley expert on sidevalve cars and Redwingers tells me that the entire Register stock of parts is 'in my garage, there isn't much, and parts are very very difficult to get'.

As to the parts covering the other cars in this book, a great quantity was liberated in the 1950s and 1960s as old bangers were stripped out to keep better examples running, and there are still strategic stocks of mechanical hardware in workshops, in garages, and coachhouses, to ensure no supply famine in the future. As Ian Gladstone told me:

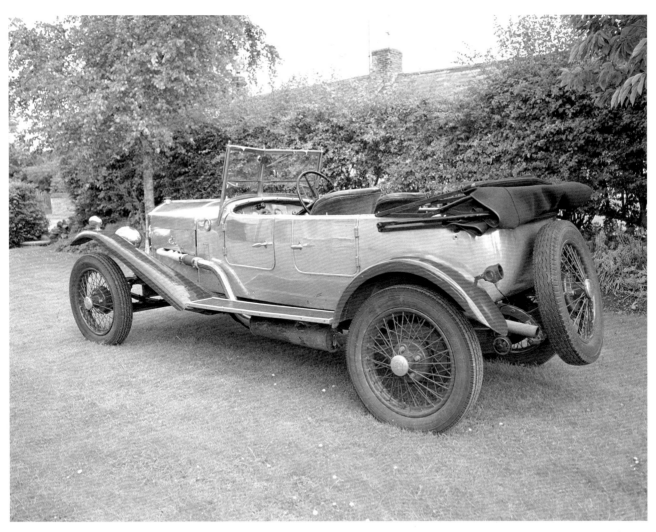

Plate 1 The four-door Redwinger had adequate all-weather protection—two-seater owners were not quite so lucky!

Plate 2 This Brooklands Nine is a very well-known ex-factory race car, registered KV 5392, showing the cycle-type wings and aero-screen used on such cars. There were no doors at first—these were added by a private owner in 1939.

Plate 3 There was *just* room in the cockpit of a Brooklands Nine for two passengers, though protection against the elements was distinctly sketchy.

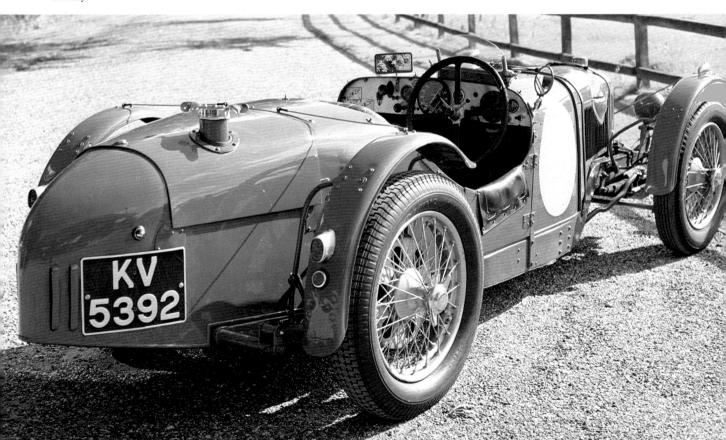

Plate 4 The race-prepared 1,087-cc engine of Richard Wills's ex-works Brooklands Nine, showing the familiar rocker cover arrangement, the twin SU carbs, and the ignition layout.

Plate 5 The familiar radiator, free-standing headlamps, and front end of one of the rare March Specials.

Plate 6 Colin Ryder's March Special was originally registered near Abingdon—and MG!—which is really carrying battle to the enemy.

Plate 7 Is a Lynx a sporting Riley or not? I think so, but I'll leave the reader to decide.

Plate 8 Some Lynxes had two doors, and some four, but all had close-coupled four-seater accommodation.

Plate 9 The Ulster Imp was a very rare racing derivative of the Imp, first built in 1934. It had an even shorter wheelbase than the Brooklands Nine.

Plate 10 The Imp of 1934 was a very smart little car, closely related in many ways to the larger-engined MPH. The problem was that it was rather too heavy for the gallant little 1.1-litre engine.

Plate 12 BLN 39, also John Gathercole's car, like the Imp, is a well-known MPH, and shows off the thoroughbred lines to perfection. Surely there's no doubt that Jaguar's SS100 was also influenced by the style of this car?

Plate 13 The side-view of an MPH is much like that of the Imp, and so it should be, for these two cars were created at the same time, in 1933-4, and share some panels and chassis engineering, though the MPH's wheelbase is longer, to accommodate the six-cylinder engine.

Plate 14 Ian Hall's beautiful black Sprite, with that characteristic 'waterfall' grille shared with no other Riley sports car. Sprites sometimes had the traditional Riley grille—this particular car has been used with both types!

Plate 15 The Sprite rear style, though clearly derived from that of the MPH, featured more flowing rear wings. The 'fin' was just for fun—but what fun!

Plate 16 Now that's what I call a *real* facia—full of instruments on the Sprite. The pre-selector gear control is to the right of the steering column.

Plate 18 Nothing complex here, but in 1924 a four-seater Redwinger driver didn't need to know any more.

Plate 19 Many Riley enthusiasts enjoy owning 'specials' in the 1980s—this one, caught at Cadwell Park, has a 15/6 six-cylinder engine, and dates from 1936.

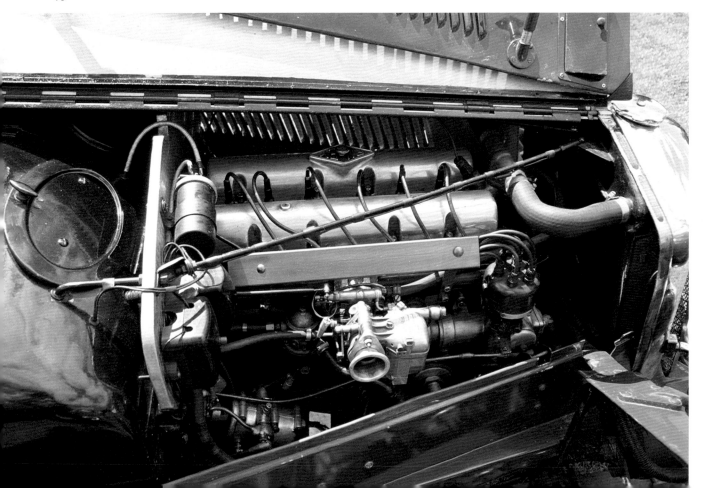

Plate 20 One of Hector Dobbs's offset single-seater racing Rileys of the 1930s, still enjoying motor sport in the 1980s.

Plate 21 A. N. Farquhar's racing Brooklands Seven, at Cadwell Park in 1985.

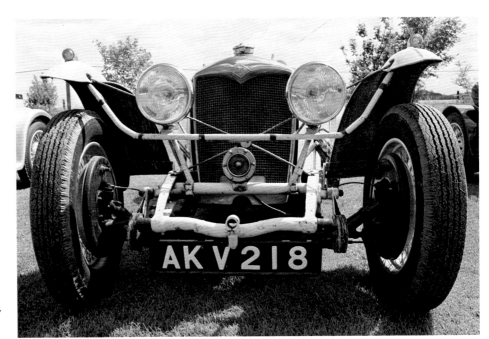

Plate 22 AKV 218 is a very famous car—being the original prototype Sprite—now much modified in the 1980s, with abbreviated wings.

Plate 23 Richard Odell's racing Redwinger in action, complete with abbreviated wings, and doorless bodywork.

Plate 24 The engine of the racing Redwinger, simple, single-carburettor, but very effective for its day.

Plate 25 Ian Hall's splendidly presented Sprite engine 'absolutely standard, old boy!', looking better, perhaps, than ever it did in the mid 1930s.

Plate 26 Sprite in action—even when trying hard they rarely roll much more than this!

'You don't have to try very hard — not unless you want the icing on the cake, and then by travelling to autojumbles all over the place, but it's not always worth it. I cleared a breaker's yard in Chelmsford a few years back, which kept me in crown wheel and pinions for a long time, but very little else except the odd axle beam, and axle case, was salvable. Good pre-war cars won't put up with sitting in the mud for more than twenty years . . .

'There are no old Riley agents to be cleared, not any more. I did get the final bits and pieces from Jordans at Godalming, but thee wasn't a lot left — I got more from the chap who had cleared them out some years before! Then I was fortunate to get the best part of Caffyns' stock from Brighton — some chap had bought the lot, stuffed it all in his greenhouse, and never used it. That was a phenomenal find.

'What usually happens is that I buy a quantity of parts, and you get some goodies and some rubbish. Sometimes I buy from an enthusiast who is getting out of Rileys, or wants to reduce the level of what he's got.'

Barrie Gillies, too, doesn't have a supply problem. In fact, looking around his workshops, and stores, his biggest problem seems to be one of finding space to keep everything:

'People ring me up, and offer me stuff. I don't actively have to hunt around any more. When I used to live in Cheltenham, many years ago, a friend and I used to share a coach-house and stables, and we used to buy Rileys for thirty bob, or a couple for £5, and we would just pull them apart to get bits for the Rileys we were actually running. We ended up with the place stacked to the eyeballs with bits. When I left Cheltenham I took my six-cylinder bits — engines and gearboxes — and left my friend with the rest. Since then he has continued to buy Rileys — they were fairly abundant in that part of the world, because there was a very active dealer — and I can still go down there and root out most parts that I need.'

Let me now turn to the restoration of various mechanical items. Naturally there are no original new chassis frames available, though a chassis can usually be straightened out unless it has been involved in a truly horrendous shunt. One of the country's biggest chassis builders, in their heyday, was Rubery Owen, of the Staffordshire Black Country, and they founded a small restoration company, some years ago, to carry out re-builds and re-creations — at a price — for those who needed that service.

It takes a lot for a Riley chassis to rot away, and most can indeed be reclaimed. The bad old days of rebuilding a frame, then stove enamelling

Compared with the MPH, the Sprite had boxed in chassis members, but the basic layout of both types was the same. Road springs were short, and stiff.

Below right: The rear end of a Sprite frame shows the boxing in, which was added to the basic MPH design. Everything you see here can be found if a major rebuild or restoration is planned.

Below: On all Rileys it is essential to keep the brake actuating mechanism well lubricated, and to keep the king pins well greased.

it, or even painting in an exotic colour, have long gone. The yellow frame in 'B. Bira's' ERA has a lot to answer for! The Riley factory, after all, slapped a very basic black finish on their production *and* race car frames — there is really no need for a restorer to go any further.

Riley sports car bodies were very simple. The Sprite (this car)/MPH/Imp body style was formed around a wooden skeleton. New panels are not available from the factory, of course, but re-manufactured components can be produced. They are not cheap.

When I visited the Gillies' workshops in Berkshire, I saw several modified saloon car chassis frames having racing-type body shells built up on them. These were all forming the basis of new Specials with Riley mechanical equipment, but as they all featured that important wheelbase figure of 8 feet 1.5 inches it follows that there could be wider implication. Barrie Gillies cheerfully admitted that such frames could be used to help rebuild a Sprite, or even an MPH, but that he had absolutely no intention of trying to fool anyone by producing absolute replicas.

The frames are created by cutting off the appropriate rear half of a mid-1930s Riley saloon chassis, which had a wheelbase much longer than required, and had side members swept up and over the rear axle line. A narrow-track 12/4 frame (introduced in the autumn of 1934, and built by hundreds) is the ideal basis for this, and the underslung rear half is entirely new.

From the Brooklands Nine to the Sprite, all the sporting Rileys had the same front and rear track measurements — 3 feet 11.75 inches — but the problem with the front axle beams is that there are several types, and one is by no means right for all types of sporting car. Fortunately the parts books for touring cars exist, and can be cross-checked, and fortunately each sporting car had a touring car of the period from which its axle beam was most certainly 'borrowed'. All the axle beams were steel forgings, and not even fifty years of neglect, and exposure to the weather, can rot them away. Making good the king pin eyes, which may have stretched, is feasible, if not exactly cheap.

After all this time one might expect major castings to be in short supply, but with one major exception — the six-cylinder block — this does not seem to have happened. Although some engine blocks are now showing signs of rust corrosion from the inside, there are still lots of Nine, and 12/4 engines available, though some need a great deal of attention before being back in first-class running order. Cylinder heads, like blocks, were cast iron, and have also survived in large numbers — over the years, however, there were various different types for various different models, so one should take care before snapping up a so-called 'bargain'.

As Ian Gladstone told me:

'I've got a lot of Riley Nine blocks, but all that glisters is not gold, as they say, and I *always* look closely inside to be sure that they are sound.

'The 12/4 is a well sorted engine, but you still have to be very careful. Internally it's a much better engine than the Nine, which had any amount of odd little pipes going everywhere; these are a tremendous source of problems.

'Incidentally the Big Four doesn't really apply to the cars you are covering, but it was an excellent engine, very well sorted, and with the minimum of clutter inside.'

Could one 'cheat', by using a post-war RM-Series 1$\frac{1}{2}$-litre engine in place of the genuine 1930s article, I wondered? One can, apparently, but the later block is not compatible with the earlier gearbox, so it really isn't worth attempting.

Until recently, the six-cylinder engines were becoming very scarce indeed:

'There was the major problem, known as the water-cooled centre bearing,' Barrie Gillies says. 'Although Riley provided a nice little drain tap on the side of the block, close to the bearing, this was sometimes not opened, to drain the water on frosty nights, by the owner. In any case, over the years lots of sludge collected in the thin water passages, and the result was that a lot of these blocks went 'pop' during the winter — either the side of the block was pushed out, or the centre main bearing pushed out, or the centre main bearing dropped out completely.

'This was so bad that in 1937, when there was a very bad winter, Riley actually re-cast a batch of blocks, using the later 15/6 pattern equipment, which doesn't have a water-cooled centre main bearing. They are now the nicest blocks to get hold of, because they have more meat round the bores'.

Nowadays, too, there is an alternative, though expensive, solution. ERA expert Donald Day had already satisfied a need among fellow ERA

owners (a select crew, to be sure!), by completely re-creating patterns for the casting of the ERA cylinder block. As every Riley enthusiast knows, this was a redesigned version of the Riley block (though without the characteristic through-the-block front mounting support system) which kept the same basic dimensions.

After a lot of hard work by Barrie and Nick Jarvis (and, it must be admitted, major errors being made with the first attempts — for the ERA block is actually a different height from head face to crankshaft centre line!) ways were found of modifying these patterns so that Riley *and* ERA blocks could be produced from the same pattern equipment. These, of course, are 'dry' blocks (for the ERA never had a water-cooled centre bearing), so owners of six-cylinder engines can now breathe again. Mind you, it isn't going to be cheap to carry out the rebuild!

Elsewhere in the high-cam engines, most components are freely available, and all components can be found — new or re-conditioned, standard-specification or modified — given time. All the Riley camshaft

When restoring a Riley sports car body, come to terms with the fact that cockpit space is limited. If originality does not matter to you, you could cheat a bit, but the purists would then frown.

Below left: Before the valve gear is added, the Riley cylinder head looks delightfully simple.

Below: Full restoration of a six-cylinder engine in progress at Barrie Gillies' workshop near Reading.

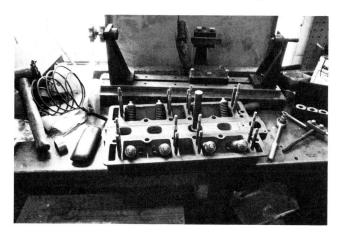

The engine on the stand is a 1½-litre Riley, the cylinder head alongside it being for a six-cylinder unit. Barrie Gillies' workshops, near Reading.

There is a healthy demand for racing Riley 'specials' in the 1980s. That is a *very* large supercharger being fitted up to a four-cylinder engine . . .

profiles, touring, sports and racing, are known, for they were simple three-arc shapes, and all can be re-created. This explains why so many Riley fanatics seem to have built high-performance specials that go equally as well as a 'works' car (if not a 'Dixon Special') ever did.

Crankshafts, connecting rods, pistons, and valve gear are also available — so a sporting Riley restored in the dark days of the 1950s when no-one seemed to care too much about them, or keeping them original, could certainly now be returned to the right level of equipment, even if that equipment was made as recently as the mid-1980s!

Modern materials, modern fuels, and all the racing experience built up in the half-century since Riley's heyday in the mid-1930s has allowed changes and improvements to be made to the surviving units, both sports and racing types. Re-manufactured camshafts tend to have different (modern-technology) profiles which give the rest of the valve gear a much easier time, and allow the lift and the overlap to be increased considerably.

Incidentally, it was not until the Dixon Specials were sold-off, after the great man had stopped racing, that the rest of the Riley world fully realised how much he changed the basic design. Not only were his single-carburettor-per-cylinder induction systems so carefully engineered (these included sliding-plate throttle controls, on nearly frictionless roller bearings), but he had re-worked the cylinder head gas-flow arrangements completely. Instead of a hemi-spherical head, he had re-developed the profile to nearer the pent-roof system which increased gas-flow around the valves, had gradually reducing diameter inlet tracts all the way up to the back of the valve, and he even ran with standard-diameter valves when the general trend was to use larger valves . . .

All things are possible for sporting Riley enthusiasts, even in the 1980s. That is a new chassis for a Sprite, or equivalent racing special, in the foreground, with a reconstructed Sprite body shell behind it. Barrie Gillies' workshops again.

[Barrie Gillies also insists that the 12/4 can be persuaded to give more power from the standard cylinder head, rather than from the big-valve Sprite-specification head.]

In general, there is certainly no shortage of gearboxes — manual or pre-selector — for the restoration of Rileys, though ENV pre-selector transmissions are rarer than the Armstrong-Siddely type. There seem to be many more spare Nine gearboxes than engines (and there are plenty of

Is it sacrilege to point out that much of the running gear of the Kestrel could be used in the restoration of a sporting Riley?

A new racing-style Riley chassis, with the first 'skeleton' stages of a body shell, on the jig. It's usually only a matter of money, and patience, to get such things done.

them). Any competent Riley restorer tackles manual gearbox rebuilds, and Gillies not only re-builds pre-selectors, but also manufactures special parts for them. The 'silent-third' gearbox clearly had quite a lot of torque capacity to spare when used behind the small Nine engine, for it also found a home, in modified form, in the Imps, and the early six-cylinder cars.

One reason, I am sure, for the use of the rather heavy and non-sporting pre-selector transmission in cars like the MPH and the Sprite was that cars like the ERA had made the pre-selector transmission very fashionable at this time. There would, indeed, be another (Borg Warner — manufactured) Riley manual gearbox in due course, but it was not available even when the Sprite was introduced in 1935/6.

Ian Gladstone can see the time ahead when supplies of the late-1920s short-pinion crown-wheel-and-pinion sets will start to fail and run out, for he notices an increased demand for replacements already, but new supplies of some popular ratios (including 5.25:1 sets) for post-1932 axles are already being re-made by the Riley Register.

On the question of ratios, most Riley enthusiasts now seem to agree that the pre-war cars were all under-geared, to follow the then-current fashion of using top gear as often as possible. (The *real* reason was that the average motorist was not good at changing gear with a 'crash' box, so manufacturers provided him with low gearing to cut down on the number of gear changes necessary. No Riley manual gearbox ever had synchromesh gears, until the Borg Warner 'overdrive' installation was introduced for 1½-litre and Big Four models in the late 1930s).

Even in the 1930s, it was possible for a customer, if he insisted, to order non-standard gearing — perhaps as high as a 4.77:1 final drive for a touring car instead of the 5.5:1 or even 5.75:1 ratio normally catalogued. As far as the twin-high-cam engined cars which we consider in this book are concerned, all of which share the same 3 foot 11.75 inch. tracks, the basic axle casings, and the basic differential designs, were all the same, as a survey of the Spare Parts Catalogues for the Nine, the $1\frac{1}{2}$-litre and the Six-cylinder models confirms.

Some of the back axles were manufactured by ENV, who also supplied the same standard axle (but often with different ratios, to Triumph and Rover, who also assembled their cars in Coventry). ENV, however, are no longer in business, so perhaps it as well that there is no shortage of supplies for rebuilds. However, I am assured that post-war RM — Series Riley crown-wheel-and-pinion sets (the ratios were 4.11:1 and 4.89:1 — of which the last ratio would be of the greatest interest to 1930s Riley owners) can be fitted after modifications are made.

The big banjo axle rarely seems to give trouble, as all items like seals and bearings are replaceable, and easily removable. Which is probably just as well, for to re-manufacture simple castings like the nose cones for the axles and — one day — for the sump pans, is one thing, but to find the money up-front to look after re-forging of the axle would be very costly. If that ever happens, I would guess that a more modern, and more freely available, banjo axle assembly like that of the early MG MGB (the track is almost the same) would be pressed into service.

In the restoration business, Rileys come back to life in many different shapes and guises — the race car side of things continues to grow.

In general, most brake and suspension parts except expanded housings are all either available from stock, or are re-manufactured from time to time. Girling are still remarkably helpful over brake parts ('just so long as their computer tells them it is still profitable' — as one cynic remarked), there is absolutely no shortage of brake drums, and the various rods, brackets, pivots and cables can all be supplied.

In these days of coil springs, and telescopic hydraulic dampers, it is also nice to know that you can still find leaf springs and (expensive) Hartford dampers for Rileys, while it is still quite feasible for existing components to be re-furbished:

'One thing that is getting a bit alarming,' Gillies remarks,' is that we now crack test stub axles, and find an enormous number of them cracked. But there really is nothing that can't be made. If the customer will pay — and wait for the job to be done — we can make it. After all, you can get *anything* for a Bugatti, which is a much more complex car in some ways — I'm convinced there are such things as new Bugattis now — so the technology and the skill is certainly available. Given a back axle casing, and a front-axle beam, you could certainly build a new Riley too.'

Restoring a Riley from the ground up is not for the faint-hearted, or the inexperienced, but at least it all eventually slots together, Meccano-fashion.

The trouble used to be that people with very little money bought a Riley — a touring Riley, probably — and thought it could be spruced up to pass the MoT tests, and have quite a bit of restoration work, for only a few hundred pounds. That was before they discovered that simple things like the king pins were loose in the axle eye, the brake linings were worn down to the rivets, and the shackle pins were worn out. They might also need new half-shafts, or hubs, if they were honest with themselves, and looking to have a truly roadworthy car at the end of the work. That was even before they began to consider the body — and they soon discovered that not even a Riley can be rebuilt *so* cheaply.

Times — and costs — have changed. It's sad, but true, that whereas the Naval cadets at Dartmouth, in the 1950s, could buy, run, and enjoy an Imp, before selling it to someone in the next intake without losing money *and* without spending a fortune on upkeep (true story, I promise you — it happened to a friend of mine, who now wishes he had not been so eager to part with the car), in the mid-1980s an Imp is really a 'collector's car', and is treated as such.

That doesn't alter my conclusions on restoration, however, which are that a sporting Riley is not only worth the effort, but that it can all be restored — at a price!

I would not recommend body shell reconstruction as a private Riley restorer's hobby, though the chassis work should be within his scope. *All* mechanical items are available — new or rebuilt.

VII
Parts and Interchangeability of Parts

One of the factors which helped to produce the individual charm of a sporting Riley was that so many of the components used in the cars were of unique design. Either they were manufactured by Riley, somewhere in Coventry, or were designed by Riley engineers and built by a supplier. If this book was about an MG, or a Triumph, I might be able to point at other more mundane, less desirable, makes of car which could be robbed to help restore the sporting model. In the case of the sporting Riley that usually does not apply.

Because the numbers of sporting Rileys built was quite limited, the company could usually not afford to do more than design special chassis and body shells, before using modified versions of the running gear already to be found in other Riley models. This, then, is the clue to the use of parts, and of interchangeability — don't look at other makes of cars (except in a few cases), but do look at other *Riley* models.

As far as the Redwingers are concerned, the story is very simple indeed, for the cars are very closely related to the side-valve 11 hp Riley family cars of the period. When these cars were put on sale, Riley boasted that everything possible was built in their own factories — except for proprietary items like tyres, and electrical fittings.

If anyone was lucky enough, therefore, to find a hitherto-undiscovered Redwinger, he should look to other side-valve Rileys for mechanical parts, and to his own ingenuity (and bank balance!) for body restoration. New body items are not available, as I have already made clear in an earlier chapter, and there is little point even in looking to vandalise another 11 hp car's body shell (except for the radiator block itself), as much of the Redwinger styles (two-seater or four-seater) were unique, and made of aluminium. The all-season four-seater Tourer of 1923 used essentially the same body style as the later four-seater Redwinger, but steel skin panels were used instead.

Except for the engine tuning details (including carburettors and settings), and Redwinger is very much like that of the other side-valve 11-hp cars, the gearbox was the same, as was the drive to the rear axle, and

the axle itself, though the final drive ratio may be different. What I am now going to say will inevitably offend some purist, but if you were to find a derelict side-valve Eleven from which the body shell had entirely disappeared, you would certainly be able to use it as the basis for most running gear parts for a Redwinger reconstruction. And why not?

Now we come to the Brooklands Nine, and it is here where the individual number of differences begin to mount up. The chassis frames and the body shells (whether for sports car racing, or for road-car use) were completely special to the Brooklands, and no other Riley can provide parts.

The engine, gearbox and transmission were all developed from those of the Riley Nine family cars of the period, and as Brooklands experts have confirmed in other places these changed considerably during the time that the Brooklands was on the market. Merely to summarise these gives an idea of the way that the Brooklands was also affected:

In the first three model years the Nine progressed through Mks I to III, the Mk IV heralded the 1930s, and for 1931 there was the Plus range, which included many detail chassis improvements. The last few Brooklands built (there were not many constructed from new parts in 1931 and 1932) may have included some 'Plus' features.

Comparing the Brooklands Nine with other Riley Nines like the

The Gamecock tourer of the early 1930s had four seats, and the body had rear seats which could be hidden away. Note the cut-back running boards which have no function except to change the looks of the car.

Three-quarter rear view of a Gamecock tourer — a touring, if not a sporting, Riley.

This Gamecock had an appropriate radiator mascot . . .

Monacos, San Remos, and Biarritz, it is easy to see that the same basic 1,087-cc engine, and the same basic four-speed 'silent third' gearbox were used, along with the same torque tube drive and location system of the spiral bevel rear axle.

In picking up any old Nine engine to use in a Brooklands rebuild, remember that every Brooklands had a water pump (driven from an extension of the magneto shaft), there was a larger capacity sump with a quick filler at the front. Some Brooklands engines had the same crankshaft big-end bearing diameters as the saloons, but later examples were enlarged to $1^{11}/_{16}$ inches (or even $1^{31}/_{32}$ inches in special blocks for racing purposes). The compression ratio was higher, both camshaft profiles were those of the exhaust side on touring Nines, and of course they all had twin carburettor (some even a four-Amal carburettor) installations.

While the gearbox used the standard casing, the Brooklands had a remote control gear change all of its own, and the gearbox ratios themselves were much closer — first gear on a standard saloon had a ratio of 3.88 inside the box, compared with 2.47 for a competition Brooklands.

The front axle and the rear axle forgings were the same as those of the saloons, and all had the same brakes as those of the saloon as well. Front and rear springs, of course, are unique to the Brooklands (particularly as the rear of the frame is underslung, whereas that of the saloons is swept up and over the line of the rear axle), though the Hartford dampers are of a type used by the Riley saloons, and many other cars of this period.

The steering gear, and much of the linkage, is the same as that of the saloons — though many surviving Brooklands have been modified considerably over the years. Most surviving Brooklands Nines have six-stud wire spoke wheels (as used on the family cars from the start of 1930 model year). The most important thing to assume about any Brooklands is that its specification may surprise the owner when he delves deeply — the Brooklands was that sort of car, and specifications differed widely from example to example.

Next, in Riley chronology, we come to the March Special, which is a relatively easy car to pin down. It was only made over a limited period —

Some Nine 'Specials' had coachwork as stylish as any produced by the factory. What about this example . . .

the 1933 model year — and all were based on the rolling chassis of the Nine of that season. Accordingly, any of the major mechanical parts found in a Nine in the 6019800–6022600 chassis number range should be interchangeable, and of course many of the cars with the same dropped chassis frame (which was introduced for the Plus Ultra cars introduced in the autumn of 1931) are also effectively the same. The engines were always Special Series, and could be found in other Riley Nines as optional extras, while the gearboxes and transmissions were unchanged, usually retaining the same ratios, these being exactly the same, and using the same gears and details, as the earlier Nines. The 'Brooklands' remote-control gearchange was also used.

It is worth noting, at this stage, that the basic front axle/gearbox/ torque tube/rear axle components introduced for the *Mk III* Nine were continued in production, essentially unchanged, for a good many years, though there was continuous detail updating which sometimes made direct interchangeability difficult to ensure.

The Imp and the MPH models, in a way, have to be considered together, if only because they were very similarly styled (using *some*, common body framing and the same centre-section fittings), and the same basic chassis design but with different wheelbases.

Considering the Imp first, it had a unique 7 foot 6-inch wheelbase chassis frame which, although based on the earlier Brooklands Six, Grebe *and* MPH layout, had unique side members. Some cross-members were the same as those of the MPH, and indeed there is evidence suggesting that the Imp was conceived in something of a hurry once the MPH had been developed.

As before, the familiar 3 foot 11.75-inch wheel tracks were used at front and rear, confirming that the same type of front axle beam, and the

. . . and its facia panel?

same spiral bevel rear axle, were used as in previous models, and indeed in the MPH. Brakes, steering, and general chassis details were all logically 'lifted' from the latest Nines.

The engine of the Imp was not as highly-tuned as that of some Brooklands, and in standard twin-SU carburetted form it was effectively the same as the Special Series engines used in the Nine family cars of the period. However, this was one of the first Nine engines to use the round-profile rocker covers, and there were once again external oil feeds to the rocker shafts.

At first the Imp was offered with a choice of gearboxes — the faithful 'Silent Third' four-speed manual transmission and standard ('wide') internal ratios, or the newly adopted ENV-manufactured 'Wilson' four-speed pre-selector transmission. The ENV box, for which more than one set of internal ratios was ever available, had been lifted to the Nine from the start of 1934 model year, just a few months before the Imp was launched, and would be used until 1935, when a change was made to Armstrong-Siddeley-manufactured boxes.

(It is important to emphasise at this point that although many British cars used this 'Wilson' transmission in the 1930s, there were three different types, one built by ENV, one by Armstrong-Siddeley and a third by Daimler, solely for their own use. The two boxes used by Riley are not interchangeable, though their principles of operation are the same. The make of each type of pre-selector box is made clear by a plate riveted to the outer casing. All pre-selector Imps used ENV-built transmissions.)

As with the other Nines of the period, the Imp featured torque tube transmission to the spiral bevel rear axle, the casings of which, and the internal shafts, were just like those of the family cars, but not found on any other marque. The Imp's final drive ratio was 5.25:1, the same as had been

Not all Nines are reconstructed as Brooklands replicas . . . but this picture shows off the Nine engine (front end), and magneto layout to perfection.

used in all normal Nines built up until the end of the 1933 model year programme. Since then, however, with Nines getting heavier and heavier as chassis and coachwork were beefed up, the touring cars had to run a 5.5:1 ratio.

The source of *all* Riley final drives, and differentials, is not at all clear. Some, for sure, were made by Riley themselves, but some were certainly made by ENV or Moss, Birmingham-based gear-cutting companies, and since these companies also supplied other Coventry concerns like Rover and Triumph, it may well be worth combing rival specifications if the supply of Riley parts (which is assured for the moment), runs out.

Riley interchangeability, over the years, is quite legendary — Barrie Gillies tells me of running pre-war Rileys with high-ratio post-war RM-Series 'Nuffield Riley' crown-wheel-and-pinion sets. Nevertheless, it isn't always wise to make assumptions. Always check with restorers, or specialists, before taking the plunge.

The MPH was built in such limited numbers that it would have been madness to make it any more specialised than necessary. It would be quite unfair to dub it a 'parts-bin' model, though there were elements of that philosophy in its design. First of all, the chassis frame (like that of the Imp) was closely related to that of the current racing Riley sports cars of the period, and not at all to any of the saloons. The MPH's frame was underslung at the rear (the rear axle rode above the line of the side members), whereas every saloon Nine and six-cylinder frame arched over the line of the rear axle.

(It was, incidentally, very much the same as the frame of the Sprite which followed, but surely no vandal would set out to destroy or to cannibalise a Sprite to rebuild an MPH . . .?)

The body shell shared its centre-section framing and panels with the Imp, and also had some sections in common with the later Sprite, which took over from it in the autumn of 1935, but was otherwise quite unrelated to any other Riley, and certainly not to any other car, of any other make.

In its running gear, the MPH was familiar, for it featured that well-known front and rear track dimension of 3 feet 11.75 inches which meant that the usual type of front axle beam, rear axle forgings, and 18-inch or 19-inch wire-spoke wheels could all be used. The brakes of the MPH, however, though operated by the Riley continuous cable method, as with the Imp and other family Rileys of the period, used massive 15-inch drums, these not being used on any other Rileys, except racing cars and some Stelvio's.

The six-cylinder engine retained its water-cooled centre bearing (some MPHs have been re-built with roller centre bearing blocks, following failure of the original casting), and was at first offered in 1,458-cc and 1,633-cc sizes, both of which appeared in the 1934 model range. This is confirmed by both the touring cars and the MPHs being in the '44T' chassis series. These were Special Series units, also found in the touring

Some Nines can be used to provide engine components for the more sporting Rileys. This is a very 'basic' single-carb engine tune, for instance, with coil and distributor ignition, and no water pump, fitted to a Monaco.

cars, and although triple SU carburettors were fitted to the touring cars, almost every MPH was fitted with a twin SU installation. The MPHs, incidentally, had special oil pump drive arrangements, valve timing, and those unique six-branch exhaust manifolds.

As with the Imps, the MPH was offered with a choice of transmissions — the Silent Third four-speed manual transmission, with the internal gear ratios found in Brooklands Nines and racing Rileys (but not in the bread-and-butter cars), or a pre-selector gearbox, this time built by Armstrong-Siddeley, and fitted with closer ratios than those boxes fitted to the touring Rileys. According to the catalogue, that is — but who has ever seen a manual-transmission MPH?

In the case of the pre-selector gearbox, there are several other cars whose pre-selectors could basically be useful in an MPH, except that many of them have the wider, and inappropriate, gear ratios. There is absolutely no shortage of pre-selector boxes, or of the expertise necessary to rebuild them, so the dire need to cannibalise does not yet arise..

Note that the catalogue (as opposed to the *best*) final drive ratios for the MPH are 4.77 (manual transmission) or 5.0:1 (pre-selector transmission), which were ratios rarely found in any other six-cylinder Rileys, or the 1½-litre models which followed. In those days gearing was for flexibility, but this meant that some cars were under-geared — nowadays, with better roads available, some cars have been re-geared, with higher ratio axles.

Finally, we come to the Sprite, which was very much more than the re-engined MPH (with a modernised nose) which some people have casually stated. Although it used *basically* the same chassis frame with the same wheelbase, this frame was much more rigid, with the side members being boxed from front to rear. The engine, of course, was completely different, but so was the braking system, and there were important (if not always obvious) differences to the bodywork.

The Monaco was one of the 'classic' Riley Nines, with a stylish four-door saloon shell. Much of what was hidden underneath featured in the Brooklands Nine, and some parts could even be used in the Imp.

Let's start with the engine, which was based on the 12/4 unit introduced in the autumn of 1934 for the 1½-litre range of cars. In the saloons, however, there was either the standard engine with a single Zenith carburettor, or the Special Series engine with twin Zenith or SUs. Power outputs were about 46 bhp, and 52 bhp respectively. Then, to confuse

everyone, the Sprite engine itself was offered in some of the touring cars from 1936.

Some aspects of the Sprite engine were the same, and of course the bore, stroke, capacity and general layout were all the same, but the Sprite had a different, more sporting, inlet camshaft profile, and slight differences to the exhaust profile. More basic, though, were cylinder head differences on most of the cars, for the valves were larger, as were the ports; later cars had higher compression ratios, and there were lightweight rocker arms. Even the water flow paths through the head casting were different; later cars had 'cross flow' cooling. For all those reasons, it is difficult to cannibalise a saloon car's standard or 'Special Series' engine to produce a Sprite top end — better by far to start from a Sprite engine itself.

The standard engine block could be used, though the 'hot-spot' cross tubes would have to be blanked off, and much of the bottom end is interchangeable, though the Sprite's 17 pint engine sump, and the oil filter body, are specially shaped and finned to encourage oil cooling. Don't forget, either, that Sprites used Scintilla Vertex magneto installations

The six-light Kestrel was a rakish mid-1930s Riley saloon style, built with several different engine tunes. This particular car is a Kestrel-Sprite, with a 1½-litre four-cylinder engine.

instead of the coil and distributor installation of the saloon car engines.

According to the catalogues, the Sprite could be supplied with a manual transmission, but almost all the surviving Sprites seem to have pre-selector transmission, in this case manufactured to the 'Wilson' principle by Armstrong-Siddeley, of Coventry. The rare 'manual' Sprites used the same basic type of silent-third gear type of transmission with the same cluster of gears as the Imp and other Nine-engined cars of the period, with a Brooklands-type remote control, though there were different bearings and constructional details.

All the $1\frac{1}{2}$-litre 12/4 models had the same basic type of pre-selector transmission, though the touring cars had different, wider-spaced, ratios, and even these were changed during the four-year career of the $1\frac{1}{2}$-litre range! The Sprite's internal gearbox ratios are very different from those of the MPH, too — but as far as rebuilding and restoration is concerned, this can all be taken care of during re-assembly.

Behind the pre-selector gearbox there is the usual type of torque tube drive to the spiral bevel rear axle, whose track is 3 feet 11.75 inches and which therefore has a lot in common with other Riley axles of the period. The Sprite's final drive ratio was 5.22:1, only slightly different from the 5.25:1 ratio found on earlier Rileys, but with a completely different combination of teeth (47 crown wheel, 9 pinion teeth, instead of 42 and 8 teeth respectively). Considering the performance that it could put up on the road, even in standard form, the Sprite must now be considered as under-geared, but the excuse was that this ratio was the same as that being

More for curiosity value than for 'interchangeability' — this picture shows one of the 1939-model 'Nuffield' Rileys, with the 16 hp 'Big Four' $2\frac{1}{2}$-litre four-cylinder engine, being used in 1940, by which time the Second World War had started. This explains the headlamp mask on the right-hand unit.

used on all other 1¹/₂-litre models built from the start-up of 1936 model year (i.e. — at the time that the Sprite was introduced in October 1935); the 5.22:1 ratio figured on 1¹/₂-litres until 1938, and was also found on late model (1937-8) six-cylinder models too.

The other big advance, for the Sprite, was that it was fitted with the latest Girling road-operated braking system, which was that also specified for the new 1¹/₂-litre cars. It follows that, if you must, there are brake parts of the saloons which could be used in a Sprite (though most parts are either available from stock, or can be re-manufactured if needed), while the same type of Girling installation was found in several other makes of car built at the same time. The 13-inch brakes were special, and different from the ordinary type, but the internals were those of the 1¹/₂-litre Riley saloons.

The Sprite's front axle was a lightweight 1934-style Nine design (the Imp was the same), the 19-inch centre lock wire-spoke wheels were the same as those used on some MPH models, had 3-inch rims, and were produced by Dunlop, who supplied such wheels to several other manufacturers at the same time. The 1¹/₂-litre touring cars, incidentally, used 18-inch diameter (later, 17-inch) wheels which, though interchangeable with those of the Sprite, would result in a half-inch loss of ground clearance, and an unsightly increase in the gap between tyres and wings.

I would never recommend robbing one Riley sports car of body fittings to help restore another, and in the case of the Sprite this would not help anyway. Although the basic style is superficially similar to that of the MPH (and, in regard to the centre section, the Imp), there are major differences. The front and rear wings, of course, are much more rounded, and all-enveloping, than those fitted to the MPH, while the rear is subtly different, and just that important bit more commodious. Riley experts also assure me that there are major differences in the centre section, too.

However, to summarise, I would say that many sporting Rileys differ from the specification which the catalogues *say* they should have — these differences often dating from the time that the cars were built. If anyone was contemplating a Riley rebuild, he should first of all ascertain what was actually in the particular car, rather than the catalogue. Even Riley restoration experts find surprises hidden under the skin.

VIII

The Men Behind The Sporting Rileys

Throughout this book there are references to various personalities, several of them carrying the Riley surname. Perhaps this is the right place to summarise who was who, which car or engine was credited to which designer, and to see what continuity there was, over the years.

As I made clear in the opening chapter, the founder of the Riley industrial dynasty was William Riley, whom I ought now to call 'Senior'. His son, William Riley 'Junior' presided over the Riley car-building concern in its early days and had five sons: Allan, Cecil, Percy, Stanley, and Victor. Victor was the eldest, and almost automatically became *primus inter pares* when all were involved in the running of the business. Victor, by the way, was more of a manager than an engineering man, for it was Percy who built the very first prototype Riley car, and it was Percy who took the credit for the ultra-modern engine design of the 1926 Nine (which influenced the layout of all the other engines later produced by Riley in Coventry).

Victor was a director of the Riley Engine Company, right from the start, and became the controlling director behind the various Riley companies by the time the Nine was launched. His father, William 'Junior', was still the company's chairman in the early 1920s, even though well into his seventieth year, although according to Vernon Barker, writing in the *Bulletin of the Riley Register,* Victor had 'become the man who made the decisions as the "front" man, both socially and financially'.

That he was not a self-publicist is proved by the sparse personal references to be found in the 'establishment' motoring magazines of the inter-war years. Not even 'The Scribe', that famous gossip-columnist of *The Autocar,* had more than a few platitudes to report in his 'These Pleasant People' spot of 23 February 1934.

Victor remained chairman and managing director up to the sudden financial collapse of the companies in February 1938, and perhaps Lord Nuffield's official biographers were less than charitable when they wrote that:

'Rileys were well known in motor racing. The company itself had taken an active part in this fiercely competitive field and the financial incubus was one reason for its getting into difficulties. It is also said that its management fell apart after the death of its founder [this *must* be wrong, for William Riley Junior did not die until 1944!], when the business passed to his five sons. "All Coventry individualists". Whatever the precise reason for its position in 1938, Riley was in danger of being wound up. Mr Victor Riley therefore appealed to Nuffield to save it, by taking it over, and he decided to do so . . . When it became a subsidiary of Morris Motors, Mr Victor Riley took charge of his old firm as managing director, and in 1939 he also came on to the Board of the parent company.'

Victor Riley, in fact, continued to head Riley until the end of 1947, when Lord Nuffield initiated a typically impulsive purge which resulted in many of the older Board members, including Riley himself, being peremptorily sacked. He took no further part in Riley, whose manufacturing base was soon moved to the MG factory at Abingdon, and died in 1958, aged 82.

Percy Riley, who was seven years younger than Victor, was the designing genius of the family, not only building the very first prototype car, but designing some of the earliest engines, and being heavily involved in the Riley company's First World War efforts. He was never close to the design of the 11-hp car of 1919 because of this, and by the early 1920s he

Victor Wallsgrove in one of the very first four-seater Redwingers, complete with aluminium panels and red-painted wings. Today it is owned by Dr. Roger Andrews.

had already started work on the radical new engine concept which was to lead to the sensational twin high-cam engine of 1926.

After this, however, little more was heard from Percy for a time (we now know, of course, that he had also been responsible for the design of the six-cylinder engine, which was a logical development of the Nine's layout, and which was put on sale from the end of 1928), except that it was clear that he was always in charge overall of the design of Riley products — engines, cars, military machinery, and all the spin-offs — unless, of course, he was over-ruled by 'Big Brother', Victor.

Such an occasion came in 1933, five years after the six-cylinder engine had been put on sale, and when the Board decided to produce an entirely new design. It has been stated that Percy wanted to continue with the improvement of the 'six', and that Hugh Rose was hired to design the 12/4 instead. As Vernon Barker wrote:

> 'Percy was over-ruled in a typical piece of maneouvring between the brothers that occurred at regular intervals throughout the firm's existence. This led to Percy's virtual withdrawal from his heavy involvement in the design side at Rileys, almost for the rest of the company's independent existence.'

Nothing, nevertheless, could ever take away his success in designing the 'PR' cylinder head and valve gear arrangement which was to serve Riley so well for thirty years. Percy died in 1941; he was only 58.

At this point, therefore, I should also mention two more designers: Harry Rush, and Hugh Rose. Rush started his motor industry career with Humber (in Coventry), at the beginning of the twentieth century, on motorcycle design, and later he joined the Calcott car concern, also in the city. Joining Riley towards the end of the First World War, he was mainly responsible for the design of the post-war range of side-valve Elevens, which were announced in 1919. At this time he was the first 'non-family designer' in the company.

Rush then concentrated his energies on the development and improvement of the side-valve range, and the very different (but superficially similar) Twelve which followed it, and although he was undoubtedly the most experienced Riley *chassis* designer of the inter-war years, he was rather overshadowed by the great publicity given to the new breed of PR-headed engines, and to Percy Riley himself.

Nevertheless, when the time came for the new $1^1/_2$-litre range to be designed, in 1933, Rush had overall charge of the new project, though Hugh Rose actually pencilled the engine itself. When Rose left the company, and the company rather foolishly decided to produce its fourth new engine design in three years (the other two engines being the 8/90 vee-8, and the larger Autovia vee-8), Harry Rush was given the job of designing the Big Four ($2^1/_2$-litre) unit.

The Big Four's original cylinder head was weird, complex, and not at all deep-breathing, but Rush drew it up that way to follow the company's latest policy, which was known as 'Hi-Charge' on other engines, and which tried to ensure hot-spotting of the fuel/air mixture before it reached the combustion chamber. The 1938 re-design, first sold to the public on the 1939 model 16-hp 'Nuffield' Riley, was much better, and was to live on until the late 1950s in 'BMC' Rileys.

Below left: Lord Nuffield talking to Mr. Victor Riley (right) and Mr. R. James at the announcement of the new Riley Pathfinder on 13th October, at the Pall Mall Showrooms of J. James, Ltd.

By the time the Big Four came along, Rush was Riley's chief designer, and was therefore responsible for the overall layout of the classically-styled and engineered RM-Series cars which were unveiled in 1946. When Riley car assembly was moved to Abingdon in 1949, and when the design office, as such, was moved to Cowley, Rush had to put up with a great deal of travelling down that fast road between Coventry and Oxford. It was on one of those fast journeys, on 23 December 1949, that he was killed in a road accident. He was 65 years of age.

Hugh Rose made his name in the motor industry by his work on semi-automatic transmissions. This sort of expertise was of great interest to Rileys at the time for they, like most British motor companies, were rushing to follow the 'easy-changing' trends sparked off by Daimler's fluid-flywheel system, and the spread of GM's new-fangled synchromesh

Above: That great character, Freddie Dixon, adding water to one of his own Dixon Special Rileys, in the 1936 BRDC 500 Brooklands race, which he won. All in all, his cars were usually considerably faster than those produced by the factory.

transmission to Vauxhall and Rolls-Royce. By this time he was chief designer at Sunbeam, then making heavy middle-class cars at Wolverhampton, as part of the Sunbeam-Talbot-Darracq group. Before he moved to Coventry, he was involved in the project design of the new small Sunbeam, launched as the 'Dawn' in 1933.

Rose, for sure, was involved in assessment of short-lived Riley experiments with the Salerni transmission (which itself included a fluid flywheel); this was first used in public in the RAC rally of 1932, announced as a production item towards the end of that year, but does not actually seem to have been fitted to a Riley production car. Then came the dispute involving a new model range which resulted in Percy Riley being shunted sideways; Rose was moved off transmission work, and commanded to produce a new $1^1/_2$-litre four-cylinder engine design! It was a constricting brief, because his firm instructions included an order to use the 'PR' type of cylinder head, cross-flow breathing, and the twin high-cam valve gear, plus a three-bearing crankshaft. Original 'Rose' features in the design, which did not last long, were the use of camshafts running in oil wells, and camshaft drive by chain — the wells were deleted during 1935 (there had been problems in removing sand from the castings in this area of the block), and the chains were replaced by a train of gears (as already used on development engines for racing purposes) after only 233 chain-drive engines had been built.

At this point Hugh Rose should drop out of my Riley story, as he moved on, in the winter of 1934-5, to work at Lea Francis — but not so! The Lea-Francis 'coincidence' is interesting.

George Leek had been one of Riley's capable managers, first as Chief Buyer, and then as a production organiser, for twenty-one years, before being appointed General Manager in 1932. Then, in 1934, Leek and Victor Riley gradually began to disagree on management matters, the inevitable result being that Leek left the company in the middle of the year.

Almost immediately Leek took control of the moribund Lea-Francis car company of Coventry, which had been a notable concern in the 1920s (building, among other models, the Hyper sports car, which won the Tourist Trophy race of 1928), but by the early 1930s had descended into receivership. Leek inspired a re-born company, Lea-Francis Cars Ltd., and engaged Hugh Rose to design new models for him, which had absolutely no connection with the previous models. On the other hand, they had a great deal to do with current Rileys!

The new $1^1/_2$-litre 12-hp Lea-Francis was unveiled in December 1937 (just two months, incidentally, before Riley called in the receiver), and was seen to have a very conventional chassis with half-elliptic leaf springs at front and rear, and the side members of the frame running under the spiral bevel back axle, Sprite style. There was a conventional four-speed gearbox, with synchromesh on the upper three ratios, and open propeller shaft drive to the back axle. The wheelbase was 9 feet 3 inches and the tracks 4 feet 4 inches — both very close, though not identical, to the latest 'wide-track' 12/4 dimensions.

So far, so good — but there was a new engine, which bore a quite startling resemblance to the existing Riley 1½-litre 12/4 unit! Why Riley did not take legal action to protect its layout is inexplicable — perhaps they had enough to think about at the time, with their own financial troubles.

Not only did the new Lea-Francis engine have a twin high-camshaft layout with pushrods and reversed rockers, lines of valves opposed to each other at 90 degrees, a hemispherical head combustion chamber, and with crankshaft assembly achieved by threading it in, from the rear, through a completely circular centre bearing housing in the crankcase, but the bore, stroke and capacity were 69 x 100 mm, 1,496 cc!

The technical advance, however, was that the camshafts were carried even higher in the Lea-Francis unit than in the Riley — actually in open troughs at the top of the cylinder block — and they were driven by a combination of primary chain, and secondary gears! So Rose had compromised from his 'failed' 1½-litre layout after all . . .

Donald Healey not only worked for Riley for a while, but rallied Rileys as well — this car was Gamecock based. Later, from 1946, his new company used 'Big Four' engines.

Peak power was 50 bhp at 4,800 rpm (almost identical to Riley 1½-litre performance), while a 72 mm bore/1,628-cc version of the same unit produced 56 bhp, also at 4,800 rpm.

Nor does the coincidence end there, for after the Second World War Hugh Rose also went on to design a larger twin-high-cam engine, the 2½-litre, which had a 2,496-cc capacity, and produced 95 bhp at 4,000 rpm. The Riley 'Big Four', may I remind you, was a 2,443-cc unit which, at the time, produced 100 bhp at 4,500 rpm . . .

None of the potted company histories every circulated, none of the historical references in magazines, and none of the reminiscences produced by Riley personalities, ever made reference to stylists, or body designers, so it is impossible to credit the shape of most of the sporting Rileys to any particular person.

The Redwinger two-seater, however, was Victor Wallsgrove's responsibility (I have already touched on his career in Chapter II), though the four-seater version was merely a refinement of the existing side-valve tourer shape. The Brooklands Nine almost certainly came about as a 'this, now this, and how about that' exercise by Thomson & Taylor when developing the prototype, which really means that Reid Railton was the 'midwife'.

All the racing sports cars from the Brooklands Six to the TT Sprites were strictly practical exercises, in wrapping as little as possible, and as light, a shell around the running gear, while still meeting the appropriate regulations, as could be arranged. (I am still amused by the idea of having long tails for 'streamlining' purposes, when the aerodynamic qualities of the front end of all these cars was simply appalling!)

The March Special, which was not an in-house Riley constructional job, was probably styled by John Charles & Sons (who built the shells for Messrs Kevill-Davies & March), with personal ideas fed into the layout by the Earl of March himself.

Finally, we come to the Imp/MPH/Sprite series of cars. Although these were all different in detail, and construction, they were all clearly influenced by the same personality, and I remain utterly convinced that it was Donald Healey, in his short stay at Riley, who wielded that influence. The cars were so different in looks from other Rileys of the period that there *had* to be a fresh, outside, influence making this possible.

Yet, for all that, nearly every Riley had a great deal more character than its rivals, and it is to those very rivals, from the period, that I must now turn.

IX
A Comparison with Contemporary Rivals

I really ought to start by considering the way in which the British sports car scene changed so much in the 1919 –39 period. Let's not forget that motoring had been confined to a pastime for the well-to-do up to 1914, and that it wasn't until the so-called 'vintage' years of the 1920s that a gradual reduction in price levels, and a gradual move from hand-building towards high-volume production occurred.

At first, therefore, the early 1920s saw a huge variety of cars put on sale, many with a great deal of character, but equally many with sturdy and

The Morris 'Bullnose' was the British market leader in the mid-1920s, by which every other car, including the Riley Eleven, was judged, and priced.

reliable habits, rather than a lot of performance. Sporting cars, at this time, tended either to be spindly and flimsy machines, with very sketchy bodywork, or exclusive (and expensive) machines with larger engines, of which the Bentley 3 litre was a perfect example.

In general, any car with sporting pretensions tended to be built in very small numbers, and tended to cost quite a lot more than the average touring machine. It was into this sort of motoring scene, which was ripe for exploitation, that Riley eventually produced the Redwingers.

A brief study of the sporting cars of the period — and, by this, I really mean those cars *sold in Great Britain* (for the Redwingers were essentially home-market cars) — throws up names like AC, Alvis, Bugatti, Frazer Nash, GN, Lagonda, Lea-Francis and MG, though some of these were out of the Riley's price-bracket, and were really not the same sort of machines at all. Whereas the Redwinger was closely based on the design of a conventional, though nicely detailed, family car, a Bugatti or a Frazer Nash was a hand-built sports machine, while a GN was really an over-grown cycle car.

Considering the basic specification of the Redwingers — side-valve $1\frac{1}{2}$-litre machines using a touring car's chassis, and priced at £495 — the most direct competition came from another Coventry-built car, the Alvis 12/50. This had evolved in a very similar manner, which tells us a lot about the sort of people who were on the way to making Coventry such an important city of the period.

The first Alvis cars had side-valve engines, dated from 1920, and were

Cecil Bianchi in a Brescia Bugatti, one of the obvious rivals to the Redwinger. Note the boat-tail styling.

followed by the overhead-valve 10/30, which matured into the 1,598-cc overhead-valve 12/50 in 1923. Although the Redwinger model and its distinctive body style came first, the 12/50 was to last much longer (until 1932, as the 12/60 model), and it can only be coincidence (allied to a bit of judicious copying, in one direction or another), that the cars looked so much alike in so many ways.

The 12/50 was more costly than the Redwinger, at £570 in 1925, and although its engine was claimed to produce 50 bhp it only had a top speed of about 65 mph. It had a longer wheelbase, narrower tracks, but very similar road manners, and in the way of things that defies all logical explanation it became considerably more popular than the Redwinger — 3,705 would be built in rather less than ten years.

The Alvis 'duck's back' style, sometimes with aluminium coachwork, was much like that of the Redwinger, as was the very rare sporting derivative of the Triumph 10/30 hp model, which was the first-ever four-wheeler from another Coventry company which had previously only built motor cycles. The Alvis was serious competition, while the Triumph was really no competition at all.

AC's 2-litre model of the mid-1920s had an advanced six-cylinder engine, with overhead-camshaft valve gear. Clearly it was the same sort of size, and styling, as the four-seater Redwinger.

AC, on the other hand, built cars in tiny quantities, but were both good looking, fast (for the period), and powerful. In the mid-1920s, the true Redwinger-rival was the 11.9-hp Anzani-engined. 1½-litre 12/40 model, which had 40 bhp, and a three-speed gearbox in unit with the back axle, but even more glamorous was the 2-litre model, first shown in 1919, with an advanced overhead-cam six-cylinder unit. This engine was to be a part of AC's engineering line up until 1962!

In the mid-1920s the Anzani-engined car was much cheaper, at £275, while the sophisticated 2-litre model was directly competitive with the Redwinger at £485; if the RAC rating had not been so high, at 15.7, compared with the Riley's 10.8, its reputation as a nicely-built and successful sporting car (which included an outright victory in the Monte Carlo rally) would have brought larger sales.

In the mid-1920s, too, there was also the first appearance of the MG marque, which was really evolved by Cecil Kimber of Morris Garages in Oxford, out of the Morris 'bullnose' chassis. This was a very unpromising base for a sporting car, for it was not nearly as well-detailed a design as that of the Riley 11 (though, admittedly, very much cheaper), and Kimber was quite determined to make it more suitable.

The first MG made in any numbers was the 14/28 Super Sports, of which perhaps 400 were built between 1924 and 1926. Its engine was a side-valve unit of 1,802 cc (and an RAC rating of 13.9), and although it represented quite good value at £350 for the open two-seater and £395 for the open four-seater, it was only equipped with a three-speed gearbox. One of the more popular body styles was in polished aluminium, with painted front and rear wings. I wonder where Kimber could have got that idea?

Triumph's first-ever motor car was the 10/20 model. Right away they produced an aluminium-bodied sports model which was a direct rival to the Redwinger. It was not a success.

The Alvis 12/50 was not only a direct rival to the Redwinger, but was also built in Coventry.

One must never be diverted by the most famous early MG, which is always known as 'Old Number One', for this — the 1925 Lands End trial car — was a one-off special with an overhead-valve engine never used in MG production cars, and it looked rather like a short-wheelbase two-seater Redwinger! It would not be until the end of the 1920s, when the Brooklands had appeared, that Riley were really to look on a current MG model as a rival. On the other hand, Riley simply could not ignore the new Frazer Nash marque, which was new in 1924, when the Redwingers were already established. Archie Frazer-Nash already had a fine reputation, having successfully been involved in the GN business, and the new 'Nash had something of the same character.

Compared with the Riley, the new 'Nash was smaller and lighter, and was equipped with an overhead-valve 1½-litre Plus-Power engine. The real difference — one hesitates to call it an innovation — was the use of a three-speed chain-drive transmission (hence the pet name of 'Chain-gang 'Nash'). Compared with the Redwinger, the Frazer Nash had more performance, and a much harder ride — it was also a whole lot cheaper, for prices started at a mere £330 for the two-seater Super Sports. On the other hand, the 'Nash' was usually fitted with rather smaller bodies than the Riley, though styles could be remarkably similar, all of which helped to give it better acceleration.

The most charismatic of all the Redwinger's most obvious rivals, however, was the Type 13 'Brescia' Bugatti, which was the very first of a long sequence of exciting models to be designed and produced at

MG's M-Type Midget of 1929 was the same size as the Brooklands Nine, but had only half the power, and half the acceleration. It was, however, considerably cheaper (£175 at first).

Molsheim, in Eastern France. The Type 13 had been launched as early as 1910, and the 'Brescia' part of its title came about following racing successes in the 1921 race held near that well-known Italian city.

Type 13s continued to be built up to the mid-1920s, and by that time they had four-valves per cylinder to add to their $1\frac{1}{2}$-litres, and single-overhead camshaft valve gear. It was no matter that these were really racing sports cars sold for road use, and that they had distinctly Edwardian looks and manners on an 8 foot 4-inch wheelbase, for they still sold for only £485 in the UK. Then, as now, the 'Brescia' was a rival which Redwinger owners respected (and feared in competition) for the standard example could do well over 70 mph, and the engine could be supertuned (at a price) to make at least 100 mph feasible — stirring stuff by early 1920s standards!

In Great Britain at this time, however, the market for truly sporting cars was both fragmented and limited, which explains why I must also mention, if not describe, other Redwinger rivals such as the Lagondas, Talbots and Swifts of the period. Each and every one sold in small numbers, and by no means all marques survived to remain prosperous in the 1930s.

By the time the Brooklands Nine came on to the scene, a series of small-engined sports cars were either being developed, or were already on sale, in Britain and Europe. Although some of them (like the MG M-Type Midget) were little more than re-bodied family cars, others like the Amilcars were purpose-built sports cars. The Brooklands Nine, like the Redwinger, eventually had some formidable competitors, and once again it was not the Riley's specification, but its price, which told against it.

The Brooklands Nine of 1928 went on sale for £395, and by the end of the decade, with the country's economy, and national prosperity, sliding quickly into Depression, the number of sports car buyers was also on the decline. A cheap showroom price, rather than an exciting technical specification, was what seemed to sell.

It's worth looking at *The Autocar* Buyers' Guide, issued at the 1928 Olympia Motor Show, to seek out the Brookland's rivals, for this is an extremely limited, though interesting, exercise. The only obvious competition came from France — from Amilcar, and Salmson — while from Britain there was the 1.1-litre Marendaz Special (only built in tiny numbers, and never *commercially* significant). Right down the scale, both in price *and* performance, was the new MG M-Type Midget, which was not actually ready to begin deliveries until the spring of 1929.

It would be quite wrong to minimise the impact of the M-Type Midget. Although the original car was really only a skimpily-rebodied Morris Minor, with an 847-cc overhead-cam engine, and cost £175, it was its development which helped to kill off the Brooklands Nine. The 'ordinary' M-Type Midget was good for a mere 64 mph, and had a three-speed gearbox, but the C-Type 'Montlhéry' model which evolved from it was an altogether more serious proposition.

The Montlhéry had an engine reduced in size to a mere 746 cc, but was optionally fitted with a supercharged engine, had a four-speed gearbox, and was priced at £575. Although that was considerably more than the £395 asked for a Brooklands Nine, it was justified by a compact little chassis (the wheelbase was only 6 feet 9 inches, and the tracks 3 feet 6 inches), and by top speeds which approached 90 mph even in 'private owner' tune.

The unsupercharged car cost £490, and probably did less than 75 mph, but both types were very suitable for racing (at Brooklands, in speed trials, and elsewhere in the UK) and did as good a job for MG's image as the Brooklands did for that of Riley. I have to say that neither car was truly suitable for sports touring, and this is reflected in the number of Montlhéry sales — a mere 44 cars in a year.

Returning, now, to the obvious French rivals at the end of the 1920s — the Amilcar and the Salmson. The obvious Amilcar rival to the Brooklands Nine was the CGS model, which had a side-valve 1,074-cc engine, and was priced at a mere £285, but there was also the more specialised CGSS. (There was also the C6 model on the market at the same time, but this had an 83-bhp, six-cylinder 1.1-litre engine, cost £695, and was probably never sold in numbers in the UK).

The CGS model was just one of the C-Series Amilcars which were built from 1920 to 1929. Like the Brooklands Nine, the CGS (GS stands for Grand Sport) had a rather spidery two-seater body style, it usually had cycle type wings, and in standard form it could probably reach 75 mph. From 1926 the CGSS came on the scene, and when I note the final 'S' stood for *Surbaisse,* which is French for 'lowered', it is clear that this was even closer to the layout of the Brooklands Nine. The power output of the Ricardo-developed engine went up to 35 bhp, the later cars had a four-speed gearbox, and one example had won the Monte Carlo rally outright even before the Brooklands went on sale. As a commercial proposition this was obviously attractive, for nearly 4,700 CGS and CGSS cars were built in only five years — Riley would have loved to see that sort of demand for their own sports cars.

The late-vintage Salmsons were remarkable sporting bargains, too, judging by the prices asked (from £265, in the UK in 1929), and by their specifications. Against the Brooklands Nine (but not for long, as the last was built in 1930), the Salmson Grand Sport two-seater had a 1,087-cc engine (*exactly* the same engine size as the Brooklands, though achieved with different bore and stroke dimensions) and was fitted with a twin-cam cylinder head. To look at a mid-1920s Salmson was to see traces of GN, which had been licence-built in France in the Salmson's earlier years, so by the late 1920s the design was beginning to look distinctly old-fashioned. Incidentally, I have seen pictures of Grand Sport Salmsons clothed in two-seater shells styled in polished aluminium panels, with red wings. What a pity Riley could not patent a colour scheme!

The fact that no new rivals to the Brooklands appeared in 1930 and 1931 shows just what a low ebb the European car market was at during this time. By the time the Imp modestly arrived on the scene, however, things

The first batch of unsupercharged MG C-Type Montlhéry sports cars were worthy rivals to the Brooklands Nine, especially in handicap races.

were looking up again. The worst of the Depression had passed in 1931, car production and sales had been increasing steadily ever since, and in 1934 the rather over-weight Imp faced considerable competition.

At the Olympia motor show of that year, not only was the Imp price listed at £298, but it had to contend with two different MGs, the Singer 9 Le Mans, the SS II, and even the hand-built Alta, most of which actually cost less than this. In the next year the Balilla Fiat added its contribution, the splendidly-engineered Rapier was added, and just after the last Imp was built the hard-riding HRG also appeared.

Because the Imp used the 1,087-cc Nine engine, and was rakishly styled, the most obvious British competition came from Abingdon in the shape of the £222 PA Midget, or the £305 two-seater NA Magnette. Neither was direct, head-on, competition, but at that price they clearly attracted the same sort of clientele. The PA had an 847-cc four-cylinder overhead-cam engine, while the NA Magnette had the 1,271-cc six-cylinder unit which was machined on many of the same tools and shared the same bore, stroke, and valve gear design.

Of course, if the Imp had ever been tested by one of the reputable motoring magazines, we would have been able to make a more telling comparison between the MGs and the Rileys — but even at the time sports car owners had to learn for themselves in a burn-up to the nearest hostelry. We do know, however, that the PA had at least as much cockpit space as the Imp (in fairness, that would not be difficult), that its engine produced 35

The Morgan 4/4 arrived at the end of 1935, just as the Imp was dying; it had a much better power/weight ratio, and was a good sports car.

bhp, and that it had a top speed of about 74 mph. The PA was quite a lot lighter than the Imp, and had a shorter wheelbase, so a typical fuel consumption of about 35 mpg was only to be expected. The PA was certainly one of the nicest-looking Midgets so far built — but the Imp had the sales advantage of optional pre-selector transmission. Two thousand PAs were built in less than two years.

The NA Magnette was at once more expensive, larger-engined, and faster than the Imp, but was still a close rival. No-one would argue about its looks, and another advantage was that the same 8-foot chassis was available with four different body styles. NAs had 57 bhp (which was quite a lot more than the Imp, though of course the MG's engine was 200 cc larger too), and a top speed of at least 80 mph. Weights were not dissimilar, so perhaps it is reasonable that 738 of all types were built in rather more than two years.

It was during the Imp's short life that the Singer sports car's reputation reached its zenith. Even during a period when Singer, as quantity producers, were steadily losing market share to companies like Standard, and the Rootes Group, they produced a series of overhead-cam engined 'Le Mans' sports cars, some with the 972-cc four-cylinder engine, and some with larger, six-cylinder, $1^1/_2$-litre units. MG, for sure, were worried by these developments, and Riley can only have been depressed by the rise of yet another Coventry (and Birmingham — for there was more than one production centre) sports car manufacturer.

A Nine Le Mans cost £225, quite a lot less than the Imp, but was good for at least 70 mph, and up to 30 mpg, while weighing only about 1,750 lb, having a 7-foot 8-inch wheelbase, and perhaps more cockpit space than the Imp. In this case, I think the Imp could outrun the Singer Nine, but of the two the Singer was probably a more manoeuvrable package. Both had disappeared within a couple of years.

What of the others, already mentioned? The Alta can be discounted,

MG's J2 of the early 1930s had only an 847-cc engine, but was easily as fast as the Imp because of its lighter weight. It was much cheaper too, at £199.50.

The MG PA, which took over from the J2 in 1934, was another direct Imp competitor, this time with 35 bhp, and a £222 price tag. The PB which followed had 43 bhp at the same price.

for although it was remarkably priced at £365, it was really a twin-cam engined racing car which *could* — if you insisted — be driven on the road. The SSII was the much larger SSI's 'small sister', and although it was most attractively priced at £260, it had to struggle hard with a 38-bhp, side-valve, 1.6-litre Flying Standard engine. There was an open four-seater version, which came close to being a sporting car, but it was only the styling, and the price, which made it even a feasible Imp competitor.

The Fiat Balilla was priced right, at £238, and looked good, if rather small, but with only 995-cc and a chassis based on that of a Fiat touring car, it was not at all as pretty or as attractive as the Imp, though it was considerably lighter. Only a few were sold in the UK. The Rapier, at £375, was too specialised (and the engine — a twin-cam — must have frightened off many prospects), but the HRG, which arrived just as the Imp was dying away, was much more in the practical British sports car tradition.

The HRG cost £395 — nearly a £100 more than the Imp — but was a rather different type of car, cast more in the Frazer Nash mould. History shows that sales of HRGs were as hard to achieve as they were for the Frazer Nash; customers, it seems, wanted more comfort, and less of the solid-riding character of these rugged machines.

The sexy MPH of 1934-5 had a very definite character, and a definite, though restricted, niche in the British market place, so it was easy to define its rivals. At £550 it was never likely to be a large seller, and it had to compete against equally esoteric cars like the AC Ace, and the Aston Martin Mk II. There was also a rather excitingly specified machine from Triumph of Coventry — the 2-litre Gloria Southern Cross (which cost £335).

Opposite page: P-Type MGs were also available with four-seater open bodies, which were more roomy than the Imp, though not as pretty.

The Ace, like the MPH, was built in tiny numbers, and for 1935 was priced at £475 or £495 depending on its specification. It had the twin assets of the fine six-cylinder overhead camshaft engine (against which the Redwinger had had to struggle, more than a decade earlier), and good styling, though its chassis was no more and no less advanced than that of the MPH, and it was not 'race bred' in the same way.

Even the four-seater, which rode on a 9 foot 7-inch wheelbase and weighed 2,500 lb, looked nice, and could achieve 80 mph. The short-chassis 16/80 sports car of 1935 had the same type of elegant styling, perhaps a touch more practical than the MPH, and certainly with more cockpit space. It boasted a claimed 80 bhp, but I don't think we'll take that very seriously, and could be had with a pre-selector gearbox. It was good for about 85 mph (very similar to the MPH), but was equally as rare — if AC built ten of these sports cars in a year they felt pleased with themselves. A few of these cars, incidentally, were supplied with supercharged engines.

In 1934 and 1935, the short career of the Aston Martin Mk II matched that of the MPH quite closely — it was built in the same period, was in the same price bracket (it cost £610), and appealed to the same, exclusive, clientele. In some ways, however, its character was very different. It was, for one thing, a considerably larger car, for the $1\frac{1}{2}$-litre overhead-camshaft four-cylinder engine had to lug around a 10-foot wheelbase.

The body styling was less modern than the MPH, for there were cycle-type front and rear wings, and a narrow cockpit, and not even any running boards to give the illusion of sophistication. Like Riley, however, Aston Martin had quite a racing reputation for pluckily using 'works' cars based on road-car components, and this helped boost sales considerably. In rather less than two years 148 Mk IIs were made, in three different body styles; 2/4-seater, four-seater tourer, and a saloon. The lightest of these weighed no more than 2,125 lb. In road tests the £640 four-seater achieved

Triumph's Gloria Southern Cross could be ordered with a 6-cylinder 2-litre engine, to make it compete with the MPH, but it wasn't as fast, nor as sporting.

81 mph, once again not a figure which embarrassed the MPH, but the lasting puzzle is why so many Aston Martins, and so few MPHs, should have been sold in this period.

Early in 1935, another potential rival appeared from another Coventry concern — the SS1 sports car — though only 23 of these 'interim' cars were to be built before they were superseded by the SS100. The SS90 had good looks, and an attractive price (£395), but a very conventional chassis layout, and at this stage the car was still hampered by the use of a Standard Motor Co. side-valve six-cylinder engine (which needed 2.7 litres to provide 70 bhp) and by the marque's 'kit-car' reputation which William Lyons at SS was trying hard (and, ultimately, successfully) to kill.

SS90s were good for nearly 90 mph and 0–60 mph in 17 seconds, which was more than a match for the MPH, though the 19–20 mpg fuel consumption was nothing to be proud of.

In summary, I do not totally understand why the MPH should have sold so very slowly. It is certain, however, that no MPH was ever taken into stock by a dealer for showroom display, and since a customer was not likely to commit so much 1930's money to a sports car without first seeing it, something of an impasse was clearly reached. Next, having seen it, some prospective buyers must have been put off by the ludicrously confined cockpit, and by the total lack of useful stowage space — accordingly they marched off to order a much more spacious Aston Martin Mk II, or ordered a hand-built, but equally elegant, AC Ace. Would the lessons be learned with the lauching of the new Sprite?

As I have already made clear, the 1¹/₂-litre engined Sprite made a very discreet, quite unheralded, first appearance in the autumn of 1935, and I

Triumph's Monte Carlo was really a Lynx competitor, rather than a rival to the MPH or the Sprite, for it had full four-seater accommodation.

The Triumph Monte Carlo of 1934 was really a Riley Lynx competitor — Donald Healey (at the wheel) was behind its development.

doubt if every possible customer even knew about its existence when the time came to place orders at the beginning of 1936. No separate description, or pictures, appeared in the *The Autocar* show numbers, for instance, and the Sprite was certainly not on show at Olympia that year.

As with the other Rileys covered by this book, the Sprite was basically intended as a home-market machine which, by definition, meant that its sales were going to be limited. As Riley had already discovered with the MPH model, cars of this size, class, and price were not in great demand; at £425 (as priced for the 1936 season), the Sprite was in the same sort of price bracket as a whole series of imported American saloons, medium sized Hillmans, Humbers and Rovers, and even the cheaper end of the Daimler and Armstrong-Siddeley ranges.

Surprisingly, in 1935 there were very few sports cars at the same price, but — ominously for Riley, perhaps — there were considerably cheaper machines on offer which were really looking for the same buyers. Three obvious competitors spring to mind — AC, MG and SS — with HRG about to join in, and BMW (called Frazer-Nash BMW when sold in Great Britain) in the wings.

Without a doubt, the SS100 (which had evolved from the SS90, already mentioned in connection with the MPH) was the Sprite's biggest rival, even though it was sold with a much larger, 2,664-cc engine. The SS100 was launched at the same Olympia Motor Show as the Sprite, given a much more obvious publicity send-off, and certainly offered remarkable value at £395.

The Singer-engined HRG came on to the scene in 1936 just as the Sprite went on sale. It had a 1½-litre four-cylinder engine, an even harder ride and more stark equipment, and sold for £395.

This was the car which made all British sports cars, including the Sprite, look old fashioned — the six-cylinder, 2-litre, 80 bhp BMW 328. Post-war, Bristol and Frazer Nash used a British copy of this engine.

MG produced their pushrod-engined TA in 1936, which had 52 bhp from 1,292 cc and cost only £222. In fairness, it was a better bargain, if not faster, than the Sprite.

Its detractors tried to shrug it off as 'just another special-bodied Standard', but that was certainly not true any more. The SS100, after all, was the first SS two-seater to have an overhead valve engine (and a smooth in-line 'six', at that), it could easily outpace the Sprite, and its significantly cheaper price tag more than made up for the extra annual licence fees which had to be paid.

In Coventry, at this time, every company's designers, and stylists, were ready to look over the wall at their rivals' products, so it is easy to pick up — and explain — some general similarities of style between the MPH/Sprite, and the SS100 styling. The SS100, in fact, was just a little bit bulkier than the Sprite, and considerably heavier, though it was only two inches longer, overall. It had an 8 foot 8-inch wheelbase (6.5 inches longer to accommodate the extra length of the six-cylinder engine), and 4 foot 6-inch tracks (six inches wider than those of the Sprite). With a 94 mph top speed, and 0-60 mph acceleration in only 12.8 seconds, it was clearly the standard by which *all* its competitors had to be judged.

As with the MPH, the Sprite had to contend with the AC Ace, and although the £525 16/80 was only sold in very small numbers, it was a real rival. The 2-litre engine meant that higher annual licence fees had to be paid, but the fine styling, and the trials successes made up for a lot of that.

Fortunately for Riley, the NA Magnette (mentioned above) was a little too small, especially in engine size, to affect the prospects of the Sprite, as was the all-new TA Midget which arrived in 1936, but the MG prices were so attractive that a number of Riley sales must have been lost to these cars.

The TA was much less of a 'proper' Midget than previous models, in that it had been designed at Cowley rather than at Abingdon, and it had a modified-Wolseley 1,292-cc engine, but since it only cost £222, could achieve 75 mph, and was backed by an energetic MG dealer network, many people forgave it everything. Naturally, as it was only half the price of the Sprite, the TA did not fight for the same market sector, but there must have been instances where those interested in trials and rallies settled for 'cheap and cheerful' rather than the more solid Riley design. The 'fashion' of buying a successful competition car was well established at this time.

The HRG 1½-litre, at £395, was head-on competition, especially as its makers made it quite clear that they looked upon their new design as a car for use in competitions. (They could not, in all honesty, look on it as a comfortable road car, for the springs were so hard that the loss of a shock absorber was sometimes not noticed for days). However HRG was always a tiny concern, and they built even fewer cars than Riley built Sprites — a total of 35 cars in the 1935-39 period!

The case of the BMW 328 is the most intriguing of all, for not many Riley fanatics realise that Victor Riley was, for a time, interested in combining the Riley 12/4 engine with the BMW 320's chassis, and talked airily of building up to 5,000 units a year, which was probably in excess of Riley's total annual output at the time.

With the Sprite of 1936 priced at £425, with 60 bhp, this meant that the SS100 model announced at the same time (£395, with a 102 bhp 2.7-litre six-cylinder engine) was a real threat. The styling, too, was similar in some ways.

MG's 1¹/₂-litre VA announced in 1937 was not truly a Sprite competitor because of its four-seater layout, but with 54 bhp, and a price tag of £280 it was clearly shooting at a similar target.

The BMW import franchise for UK sales had been gained by AFN of Isleworth, the manufacturers of the Frazer Nash car, and the controlling genius of that concern, H. J. Aldington, first suggested that Riley might build the 320 saloon under licence. The idea of marrying the 12/4 engine to that car developed later, but it now seems that Victor Riley was not backed by his fellow directors in this project, and his enthusiasm died away during 1937.

In the meantime, BMW's sensational 328 sports car was launched in 1936, and AFN made plans to sell it in Britain, badged as a Frazer Nash-BMW. The first car arrived in the autumn of 1936, but sales to customers, at a price of £695, did not begin until mid 1937, by which time interest in the Sprite was at its peak. Although the BMW was considerably more expensive than the Sprite — 64 per cent more, in fact — and used a sophisticated 80-bhp 2-litre six-cylinder engine, it was a very similar size, for the wheelbase was 7 feet 10.5 inches, and the car weighed 1,830 lb.

The BMW's biggest technical leap forward, apart from the engine itself, and synchromesh gears, was the use of a rigid tubular chassis, and independent front suspension. The styling, in many ways, was similar to that of the Sprite (the two cars had similar grille outlines), except that the headlamps were fared into the wings, and the BMW had no running boards under the doors.

All in all, a total of 461 328s were built between 1936 and 1940, of which 46 were sold in the UK as 'Frazer Nash-BMWs'. Only 15 of·these cars were delivered before the end of 1937, which means that Sprite sales could not have been seriously affected, yet for Riley, and for all other sports car makers in this size and class, the 328 was an extremely important model. All realised that the traditionally-styled and engineered type of

'British' sports car would soon be rendered obsolete. Companies like Aston Martin and SS-Jaguar made haste to modernise their cars, while others, including Riley, dropped out of the race altogether.

The combination of rivalry from modern designs and tthe company's overlying financial problems, meant that Riley allowed the Sprite to fade away, unlamented. The days of the sporting Riley were at an end.

The significance of this picture is that it is of a post-1945 Lea-Francis two-seater, which was fitted with a 1½-litre or 1.75-litre engine looking remarkably like that of a Riley, and designed for this Coventry-based concern by . . . Hugh Rose!

X

The ERA Connection

In the 1930s, and even in the late 1940s, the ERA was Britain's most successful single-seater racing car. The ERA was born because of Raymond Mays' burning motor racing ambitions, and there was a strong Riley link at first. Even though ERA engines gradually became more and more specialised, as they became more and more powerful, they all originally evolved from the six-cylinder, twin high camshaft, Riley unit, found in road cars like the MPH, and in the racing machines.

The initials ERA stand for English Racing Automobiles Ltd., which was a company set up in November 1933, with one principal purpose in mind — to produce a world-beating voiturette racing car. Almost all the finance was provided by Humphrey Cook, a wealthy young man who had started motor racing in 1914, had bought an ex-works Vauxhall 3-litre TT car to go hill-climbing in 1923, and had soon struck up a firm friendship with another then-Vauxhall driver, Raymond Mays.

The Riley connection, however, was forged somewhat earlier, when Mays and his designer friend and colleague, Peter Berthon, were casting around for a new hill-climb and racing car to take over from their ageing 'Villiers Supercharge' special (which was really the ultimate development of the TT Vauxhall, which he had bought from Humphrey Cook).

It may be no more than coincidence that in 1932 Mays had bought a six-cylinder Riley Alpine saloon, direct from Victor Riley, purely for road use — especially as his intention in 1932 had been to develop a new and entirely special 5-litre Invicta racing car, with financial backing from Humphrey Cook!

At the end of 1932 Mays, as ever, was in financial trouble caused by a combination of more ambition than money, broken racing cars all around him at Bourne, and reluctant motor racing sponsors — but with the old Villiers finally re-prepared, there was time to think ahead. As Mays wrote in his famous book *Split Seconds* (now long out of print from G.T. Foulis):

'One day, as we drove from Eastgate House to Birmingham, Peter and I discussed the Villiers, Shelsley Walsh, foreign racing cars, and the

possibility of ever building a really worthwhile 1 1/2-litre British racing car.

'Riley's had worked hard and done well in sports car racing, and the possibilities of their assistance simultaneously flashed through our minds. I knew and liked Victor Riley, and there and then I decided that we would call on him that very day as we passed through Coventry. If only we knew that the 1 1/2-litre Riley engine was suitable for modifications and supercharging, we could tempt Victor Riley with the possibilities of obtaining the Shelsley Walsh record on an English car of only 1 1/2-litre capacity — and a Riley at that . . .

' "VR" was in, and would see us . . . and sitting behind his desk he listened intently to all I had to say . . . I told him of my longing to build a really fast 1 1/2-litre English racing car which could regain the Shelsley record. He was definitely interested and suggested that Peter should at once go and examine the inside of the Riley 1 1/2-litre six-cylinder competition engine to see if he considered the idea feasible. "VR" sent for that very capable engineer, his brother, Percy Riley, and with him we examined and discussed the basic design of this engine, and the possibilities of modifying it for our purpose.

' . . . "VR" asked what brake horsepower we thought the engine would give, and after a few minutes' consideration, Peter replied, 150.'

In a *really* good fairy-tale, of course, it would have been the work of mere days to tune up the existing engine, discover just how powerful it could be, and produce a world-beating unit. But this was real life, and much more sheer hard graft was involved. Nevertheless, because the Riley

The predecessor of the ERA racing car was the famous 'White Riley', which survives to this day. It was built up on the basis of a 1933 TT-style chassis, so there are obvious family connections to the MPH and the Sprite which followed. Kay Petre (seen here, at the wheel) eventually bought it from Raymond Mays, and painted it light blue. Illogical!

engine was not only sturdy, but because it basically had a very efficient cylinder head and breathing arrangements, the job was done in the end. By mid-1933 that famous ERA ancestor, the White Riley, had been born.

According to Dennis May, who reviewed the White Riley project in the *Riley Record*, in September and October 1944:

'Inside a matter of hours, during which numerous bits and pieces of engine were scrutinized and pored over from every angle, the pair from Bourne were en route for home again with a firm promise of the necessary support in cash [Mays had asked for £1,000, a not inconsiderable sum in 1932 currency] and kind, and a cubby hole full to bursting with drawings.

'A week or two later a second meeting was convened, whereat Berthon and Mays presented the Works with a detailed schedule of requirements, giving in exchange an assurance that the $1\frac{1}{2}$-litre Riley Six, modified as indicated by them, would clamber up Shelsley inside current record time, accidents barred. By this time, however,

Raymond Mays proudly poses with the original 1934 ERA, chassis number R1A, which used a much-modified version of the $1\frac{1}{2}$-litre Riley six-cylinder engine.

The ERA engine, as can be seen, filled the bonnet of this race car. The big supercharger is at the front of the six-cylinder block . . .

Mr Victor wanted to go a stage farther; his proposal — readily accepted — was that the "guest artists" should go to work on three cars instead of one, two unblowns and a blown, the former, if successful, to constitute the basis of a marketable TT type.

'But as matters were to turn out, the building and development of the famous White Riley — i.e. the supercharged sprint car — took up so much time that the unblowns never reached finality . . . '

Put in more prosaic terms, what happened eventually was that Mays and Berthon produced the White Riley on the basis of an 8 foot $1\frac{1}{2}$-inch wheelbase chassis originally designed for use by the factory in the 1933 Tourist Trophy race. This chassis, incidentally, was one of a batch of seven, two of which became prototype MPH road cars, and two others which were sold to Freddie Dixon to become 2-litre 'Dixon Specials' — distinguished company, indeed!

All the basic running gear was that of the contemporary TT Six racing sports cars, and thus closely related to that of other Riley sporting cars of the period. The most modified item of all was the engine which, while still recognisably Riley-based, was different in many ways.

In regard to the engine, 'VR' had given Mays and Berthon a free hand to make whatever modifications were necessary, except that the cylinder block should be left absolutely standard, and that the finished article should at least look like a Riley unit. The proof of the basic quality was that a great deal of power was obtained while retaining the standard block, and re-designed crankshaft still running in only three main bearings. Riley, by the way, insisted that the water-cooled centre main bearing — a roller bearing of colossal proportions — was retained.

Tom Murray Jamieson, an acknowledged supercharger expert, was invited to develop that part of the equation, while Berthon himself designed a new cylinder head which retained all the familiar Riley layout details, including valves opposed at 90 degrees. However the new casting was in aluminium alloy, while the ports were rectangular in section. The standard 6.5:1 compression ratio was retained, and a maximum blower pressure of 18 psi was envisaged. To hold down the head against fearsome combustion chamber pressures, there was a positive forest of holding down studs — a feature which Jamieson was to adopt when he went on to design the supercharged twin-cam Austin 750s later in the 1930s.

Jamieson devised a new Roots-type supercharger, which was vertically mounted at the front of the engine, and driven at 1.8 times engine speed by bevel gears on the nose of the new crankshaft. It was fed by a single, large, SU carburettor. There was dry sump lubrication, the pressure pump for which was also driven from the front of the crankshaft.

All the design, manufacturing, and development work took time, so it was not until mid-summer of 1933 that all was ready for bench testing. Plans to enter two un-blown engines in the Riley 'works' cars in the Isle of Man's Mannin Beg race were dropped at a late stage, and in fact the White Riley did not appear in public until August Bank Holiday, at Brooklands. Indeed, it should never be forgotten that the White Riley's reputation, as the fore-runner of the ERA racing car, was founded on just three Brooklands 'Mountain' races, and one Shelsley Walsh hill climb — all held between August and October 1933!

The chassis incorporated modifications to the back axle, the four-speed manual transmission, the clutch and the suspension, but was still recognisably a Riley Six. The engine was first run up (at the Riley factory in Coventry), in July 1933, and on its very first full-bore power test, it produced 147 bhp at 6,500 rpm — which was within a whisker of Peter Berthon's prediction, all those months ago, and had been developed before final settings of carburettor and timing details had been developed. The boost pressure to achieve this figure had been 12 psi, and it was quite clear that there was more to come.

In initial track tests, Raymond Mays found that the engine was quite willing to run up to 8,000 rpm — a quite unheard-of figure, so far, for a twin high-cam Riley — and in due course the power output was finalised at 160 bhp at 7,500 rpm, using the full 18 psi boost. By comparison with anything previously achieved in a British $1^1/_2$-litre machine, this was an astonishing figure, and one of which Riley could be proud.

Even so, virtually no durability running had been completed on the one and only engine before the White Riley (so named because of the cellulose paint finish used on the stark, light-alloy, body shell) was entered for its first event.

On 7 August 1933, Raymond Mays set the White Riley to its first test — the Byfleet Senior Mountain Handicap race at Brooklands, a mere six-miler, but one where every ounce of ultimate performance was needed for the short race. The White Riley started last, on 'scratch' (for its reputation had gone before it, and Brooklands's ace handicapper, A. V. Ebblewhite, was taking no chances). As Mays later wrote:

'The little car fairly screamed round the Mountain course, and I was thrilled with her performance. Alas, the thrill was of short duration, because after completing the first few laps the super-charger whine

Perhaps not many traces of the six-cylinder Riley ancestry remain obvious, but the link was most certainly maintained. Fuel/air mixture from the front-mounted supercharger was along the simple gallery.

ceased and all the power seemed to disappear. Back in the paddock we found that the supercharger drive had sheared. This was certainly disappointing but we were in no way downhearted, knowing that such a breakdown betokened no fundamental fault.'

Teething troubles, indeed, but these were only to be expected. Incidentally, the car's legend had already begun to outstrip the facts. *The Autocar's* 'Sammy' Davis wrote in his race report that 'Popularly, it was rumoured that this car's blower pressure was at least sixty pounds.' Can he *really* have been serious?

The engine was modified and rebuilt in good time for the Shelsley Walsh hill climb meeting in September where, weather permitting, Mays intended to have a crack at Hans Stuck's record, which had stood, unbroken, at 42.8 seconds, since 1930. This time, thankfully, there was no mistake. The weather was perfect, and with twin rear wheels fitted, the beret-clad Mays hurled the small car up the twisting Worcestershire incline in 42.2 seconds. At a stroke he had paid back his promise to 'VR', and 1½-litres had defeated the massive Austro-Daimler's achievement.

That was the good news. The bad news was that Whitney Straight, in his new 3-litre Maserati, was also in a record-breaking mood, and soon eclipsed the White Riley's achievement with a time of 41.4, seconds reducing it on his second run to 41.2 seconds.

Nevertheless Mays and Berthon had made their point, and the Riley concern were delighted. Before the season ended there was a chance to notch up a real racing success, at the home of British motor racing, Brooklands.

In the final meeting of the year, held in October, the White Riley was entered in two Mountain events on the same day. In the first event, it was to run against such formidable competition as Piero Taruffi in a 2.3-litre 'blown' Bugatti, Whitney Straight's Maserati, Sir Malcolm Campbell's 4-litre Sunbeam, and the Hon. Brian Lewis's supercharged eight-cylinder Alfa; it was also a 'scratch' race, which meant that all this now-priceless machinery hurled into the first hairpin bend in one terrifying mass!

It all started well, with the White Riley up in second place after a first lap sort-out at that first corner, but almost immediately the engine's distributor arm, shattered by the high revs used, brought the engine to a halt. No matter. The offending component was changed, the car went straight out, later in the day, to compete in the Oxford-versus- Cambridge Mountain race. The competition wasn't as fierce, but in the end that didn't matter, for the White Riley rushed round the course to win, off scratch, by 500 yards. The race speed was 71.39 mph, and — more important — the car set a new 1½-litre Mountain record, at 74.69 mph. It was exactly the impetus the Mays-Berthon equipe needed, for they had greater things in mind for 1934.

The White Riley's career was by no means over, after such a busy and

This is ERA R6B, with a modified nose, and now fitted with independent front suspension, as seen at Cadwell Park in 1985. It has a 2-litre version of the famous supercharged engine, like many latter-day ERAs.

successful beginning (not only would Raymond Mays use it again in 1934, when Whitney Straight's newly-imported 3-litre Grand Prix Maserati would always be the principal competition, but it would be sold to Ms. Kay Petre in 1935, and go on to further exploits), but it was soon overshadowed by the car which evolved from it — the ERA.

The White Riley, incidentally, was bought by Percy Maclure in 1937 (his father was an important Riley executive, of course), though he used the car very little. In 1939, in fact, the supercharged engine was transferred to one of his special racing Rileys, which had independent front suspension, but later in that year a powerful 'blown' engine (it *might* have been a B-Type ERA unit) was fitted to the White Riley, for Maclure to beat Mays' Shelsey Walsh time by 0.55 seconds.

Then came the Second World War, when the car was stored, and in the years which followed it was given an unsupercharged $1\frac{1}{2}$-litre racing unit, registered and used on the road, and eventually completely restored in the 1970s. Famous old cars, it seems, never die!

By the end of 1933, however, Raymond Mays and Peter Berthon had rapidly moved on from their White Riley project. As Mays wrote in *Split Seconds*:

'I was just about to arrange to see Victor Riley to discuss future plans when a letter arrived for me from Humphrey Cook, the results of which altered the whole future of British motor racing. In brief, this letter conveyed that Humphrey had watched with much interest the performance of the Riley, and that from what he had seen he considered that the engine was good enough to be used as the basis for a new $1\frac{1}{2}$-litre British racing car . . .'

What is interesting here, if Mays's recollections were clearly written down by his literary 'ghost', Dennis May, is that Cook was only really interested in the Riley's engine, and not the rest of its design. That is certainly no slur on the reputation of the Riley racing chassis, but it confirms that Cook was keen to see a purpose-built single-seater racing car designed, where chassis, suspension, and general layout were not circumscribed by the enforced use of existing Riley hardware.

(By this time, too, it was becoming clear that Riley engineers still had a lot to learn about the building of racing cars. Freddie Dixon, having purchased a car from the factory, had taken it back to Middlesborough, gone through the layout like a truly dedicated mechanic, and made a much better machine out of it. Britain's motor racing business was a small one in the early 1930s, and the word had already got around.)

ERA R8C, another 1936 model subsequently equipped with independent front suspension and the 2-litre engine, booming its way up Prescott hill climb on a filthy day.

Cook, for sure, was serious, as Mays confirms:

'Further, he suggested that, if we were interested, Peter and I should meet him with a view to the three of us forming a company to build a car to represent England internationally. He added that if everything could be arranged satisfactorily he would be prepared to finance the company . . . A meeting took place, and there and then it was arranged to form a company to build and run a team of racing cars, and if successful, to make a few additional cars for sale to approved drivers.'

Mays, although the glamorous driver, personality, and front man, had very little money of his own, so both he and Berthon had a purely nominal shareholding in ERA Ltd., but both were to be paid salaries, and while Berthon would be much involved with design and development, Mays himself would do all the wheeling and dealing needed to fix up oil and accessory contracts. Further, he agreed to hand over all rights to use the

Raymond Mays (what, no helmet?), in ERA R4D, complete with twin rear wheels, and Zoller-blown 2-litre engine, setting a new Shelsley Walsh record of 37.37 seconds, in 1939.

JCC 200 miles race start, Donington Park, 1937, with at least seven ERAs in the frame. There is also a Riley (No. 6) in the third row. Arthur Dobson (No. 9) was the eventual winner.

White Riley engine, to the new company, as a basis for the new car's power unit.

The most important immediate decisions to come out of this initial meeting were to approach Reid Railton, of Thomson and Taylors (at Brooklands) to design and build the chassis, and to approach Murray Jamieson to build and produce the superchargers. Jamieson's prowess has already been mentioned; in the case of Railton it is only necessary to say that he was T & T's celebrated chief designer (having worked with the late Parry Thomas in the 1920s), and that he had already been responsible for the successful re-building and re-engining of Sir Malcolm Campbell's famous 'Bluebird' Land Speed Record car, and for the design of the new Napier-Railton long-distance track and record car, which had just started its career for John Cobb.

English Racing Automobiles Ltd started operating as soon as possible after that meeting, with a new factory building being erected in the orchard of the Mays family home in Bourne, Lincolnshire. Mays personally negotiated with Victor Riley about the use, modification, and development, of the six-cylinder engine; until ERA's own small machine shop was ready, it was necessary for Riley to undertake the manufacture of many special items on ERA's behalf.

The ERA engine which took shape during the winter of 1933-4 was considerably different from that of the White Riley 'prototype'. In fairness, I would say that there was very little actual 'Riley' now left in the engine, except for the general layout and principles of valve gear operation! Whereas the original White Riley engine had used a completely new cylinder head casting, but had retained the Riley's cast iron cylinder block, the ERA engine now had a much changed cylinder block as well. Couple to this the use of the special Jamieson-designed crankshaft, the Jamieson supercharger, and the special camshaft profiles, and the utterly special nature of the engine becomes apparent.

As with the White Riley engine, however, there was dry sump lubrication, a single SU carburettor, and the Roots-type super-charger sucked fuel-air mixture through the carburettor before pushing it through into the engine. The blower pressure was now to be 15 psi.

Even in the beginning, ERA were considering building two different engine sizes — 1.1 and 1.5 litres, — and before the first car was shown to the public in June 1934 a third possibility — 2 litres — had also been added to the project. The $1\frac{1}{2}$-litre unit, clearly, took the foremost priority, because this would make the ERA an ideal machine for *voiturette* racing, but the 1.1-litre version would be useful for 1,100-cc races and handicap events, whereas the 2-litre (which was the largest possible 'stretch' for this engine) would offer more power *and* torque for hillclimbs, sprints, or free formula races.

Different sources quote different dimensions for the bore and stroke of the various ERA engines, but these are all very close (and probably come from different assumptions about Metric or Imperial dimensions, and the

All manner of artificial corners were applied to make the racing at Brooklands more interesting. This was the International Trophy race of 1939, and four ERAs are following a supercharged twin-cam Austin Seven through the wattle-fence chicane.

conversion from one to the other). I will merely quote, without comment, those listed in the authoritative ERA history produced by David Weguelin:

Type	Bore and stroke (mm)	Cubic capacity (cc)
1.1-litre	57.56 x 69.8	1,088
1.5-litre	57.56 x 95.20	1,488
2.0-litre	62.81 x 107	1,980

In later years, there were the following derivatives:

1½-litre (E-Type ERA)	62.81 x 80.00	1,487
1.8-litre	62.81 x 95.20	1,770
1.8-litre	64.0 x 95.20	1,838

To put all these figures in perspective, I should note that the 'standard' Riley 1½-litre bore and stroke were 57.5 x 95.2 mm, and 1,486 cc as used in Racing MPHs and TT Sprites. The Riley cylinder block was not capable of much boring out, though TT Sprites occasionally used a 63.5 mm bore, and although increasing the stroke is not usually the most ideal way of enlarging an engine, it was sometimes done, for the 2-litre TT Sprites had a stroke of 106 mm.

For the ERA application, therefore, Peter Berthon had produced a new cylinder block casting, in which the familiar Riley engine mounting cross-shaft had been eliminated. Two cylinder bore dimensions ('standard' and bored out) and three different crankshafts were needed to produce the choice of power units for the car, though externally they all looked the same. The E-Type ERA engine of 1939, combined the enlarged bore of the 2-litre engine with yet another special crankshaft.

Even Riley fanatics must have looked askance at the power outputs projected (and largely achieved, in practice) for the ERA engines. Berthon postulated 170 bhp for the 1½-litre, and 120 bhp for the 1.1-litre; the first 1½-litre engine produced 166 bhp at 6,500 rpm. The first 2-litre engine was not ready until the second half of 1934, when it produced 230 bhp at slightly lower revs than the 1½-litre.

The ERA's structure, of course, was completely different from that of any Riley, though the same basic type of four-speed Wilson pre-selector transmission (made by Armstrong Siddeley) was used. The chassis frame itself was considerably narrower than that of the White Riley, though the basic suspension layout was the same, including the retention of torque-tube transmission from the Wilson gearbox to the back axle casing proper. The side members of the frame swept up and over the line of the rear axle.

The bodywork was a true single seater, but because the seat itself had to be on top of the torque tube the driver sat considerably higher than in the White Riley or any other contemporary Riley competition car. The body shell was built entirely of light alloy, and almost the whole of the gracefully-pointed tail was full of petrol tank.

When Laurence Pomeroy produced his monumental work, *The Grand Prix Car,* he not only pointed out that the Riley-based engine was extraordinarily compact (for the main engine casting was only 18 inches long), but that each trio of cylinder bores were siamesed (there being no water between them to aid cooling). All of which made the production of really high power outputs, with reliability, quite remarkable. Pomeroy, indeed, suggests that individual $1\frac{1}{2}$-litre engines were persuaded to give 190 bhp at 7,500 rpm in due course!

The success story of ERA racing cars has been told in detail in many other publications (quite superbly, of course, in David Weguelin's ERA book), so I will merely summarise the development changes made to the Riley-based engine during those years.

The 1,100-cc engine was left behind, not only in development, but in 'fashion' terms as the years passed by — the records show, for instance, that only two cars (R2A, a 1934 'works' car, and R4A, built for Pat Fairfield as the first 'private owner' car) were 1.1s in the first place. Much of the work, therefore, was concentrated on the large capacity engines, which needed to produce more and yet more as new cars were produced by the opposition.

The major advance, first tried on an 1,100-cc engine, was to use a different, larger and more efficient type of supercharger. Instead of having the vertical Jamieson-built Roots-type component at the front of the machine, a Zoller vane-type supercharger was mounted at the rear of the engine, driven by gears from the crankshaft, and mounted above the gearbox. This allowed the supercharger pressure to be raised from the 15 psi of the Roots type, to no less than 25 lb.

This, and other related changes, allowed the $1\frac{1}{2}$-litre's power output

A curious lack of spectators at Donington Park in 1937 for this race between two ERAs . . .

to be raised to 225 bhp at 6,500 rpm right away, but well before the end of the 1930s this peak had been raised yet again, to no less than 268 bhp at 7,500 rpm! Similar, though perhaps not as spectacular, gains were made with the 2-litre unit, for Raymond Mays wrote that the original unit used in his famous R4D ERA, developed 340 bhp at 6,500 rpm! Compare *that* with the power output of the original six-cylinder Riley of less than a decade earlier.

The much more modern E-Type ERA design, first seen in 1939, used a $1\frac{1}{2}$-litre engine, though with the cylinder bore of the 2-litre engine allied to a new crankshaft stroke, and this was initially rated at 250 bhp at 7,000 rpm, and in this guise the Zoller blower was mounted alongside the cylinder block/crankcase, rather than behind it. David Weguelin claims that in its later, post-war, development stages, that output had been further boosted, to 330 bhp at 7,500 rpm.

Returning, now, to the Riley links which were retained with ERA, I should also mention that Riley machined the ERA cylinder blocks, and carried out part-assembly of the units, after which they despatched them to Bourne for the unique ERA cylinder heads and all the 'plumbing' to be attached. There was much two-way traffic of personnel, experience and ideas between Riley in Coventry, and ERA in Lincolnshire, which must certainly have allowed Riley to build more and more powerful competition engines later in the 1930s. The performance of the TT Sprites, the Freddie Dixon 'specials', and other related cars bears this out.

The pity of it all was that at the very period in which ERA's super-tuning experience of supercharged engines became available, British

. . . perhaps they were all near the start-finish line?

sports car racing was going through a period when supercharged engines were banned!

For the record, a wealthy private owner could buy an ERA, in 1935 or 1936, for £1,500 (1.5-litre), £1,700 (1.5-litre) or £1,850 (2-litre), and of course he could also buy spare, or different-sized, engines to allow his car to be used in more than one category. A total of 20 ERAs of all types were constructed — 17 of the classically-styled 1934-variety: A-Type, B-Type, C-Type and D-Type — and three of the very different E-Type machines.

All but one of the ERAs still exist, and most are still raced regularly. Having enjoyed a new lease of life in post-war Great Britain, many were passed on for use in hillclimbs, and they later came back to prominence in historic racing. Even the one missing ERA — R3B, which had been written off in an accident in 1936 — is being re-created by ERA-expert Tony Merrick from original parts.

The ERA fraternity has seen to it that none of the cars rots away from lack of use, and a batch of new cylinder blocks has been cast to make sure that blow-ups are not terminal (thought they will always be expensive). Since everyone likes lots of power, and since capacity limits do not apply to historic racing, nearly half of the ERAs now have the full 2-litre engine units.

Incidentally, don't let your mind merely boggle at the thought of a full-house ERA engine being fitted to a sporting Riley — it has been done, in relatively recent years, and the result was as exciting as you might imagine!

XI
The Riley Clubs

The Riley club spirit, like the Riley car, goes back a long way, and it has been essential to the continued life of the Riley motor car. When Rileys were made by the Riley family there was no problem, but once the marque disappeared into the maw of the BMC group, it needed all the help it could get. Today it wouldn't be too much of an exaggeration to suggest that very few vintage and thoroughbred Rileys would have survived if there had not been club enterprise, expertise, and enthusiasm to keep them going.

The story of the Riley clubs — for there are three thriving organisations in the UK, as well as local groups in several overseas countries — is not merely one of present-day activities, but of a long tradition of service to Riley owners. I'd better make it quite clear, right away, that there are two clubs to be considered in the context of 'Coventry' Rileys: the Riley Motor Club, and the Riley Register. It isn't accurate, or enough, to say that the Register only looks after 'real' Rileys, and that the Motor Club looks after everything *including* the 'BMC Rileys' — but it's a start. In the early days of motoring the only motoring clubs that mattered were the AA and the RAC (and they grew up, mainly, to defend the private motorist against the sometimes vindictive police and magistrates' courts of the day!)

The clubman's story begins in the 1920s, when the Riley marque was already thriving, and when Riley was one of the most important car-making companies in Coventry. The very first one-make club of all was for Jowetts, but this only beat Riley by a matter of months.

The spark came after the London–Edinburgh trial of 1924, when the eleven Riley crews who had entered the event were invited to supper by directors of the Riley company. A Riley club was not actually founded at that time, but club historians have no doubt that the companionship germinated on this occasion — and the obvious encouragement given by the Riley company itself — was important.

The Riley Motor Club was actually founded in 1925, at the end of the next MCC London–Edinburgh Trial, an event in which more than 20 Riley owners took part. *The Autocar* reported on the trial, writing that:

There are so many ways of juggling Riley components that many owners did it for themselves. This is a late-1930s 12/4 sporting special, obviously in need of spare parts!

'The Riley contingent, in fact, was numerous enough to have arranged a Riley celebration dinner, the only absentee of the 21 Rileys which started being A.J. Phippen's car, which broke a timing chain at Hawes.' The Riley marque won more awards than any other on this run — 19 gold awards, and one silver — and among the 'names' driving the cars were Victor Riley, Victor Wallsgrove, Cyril Whitcroft, and Victor Leverett.

This is what a commemorative leaflet recently produced by the Club says about the occasion:

'There was naturally great enthusiasm among those present which was enhanced by the unqualified success of the Riley entrants and when, at the end of the meal, speeches were made — the first by Mr Victor Riley Senior (who incidentally, never missed one of these events in the years that followed) a proposition was put forward by Mr Arthur J. Salmon that a club for Riley owners should be formed.

'This proposition met with an enthusiastic and unanimous reception, and without more ado the meeting elected the first officers — Mr William Riley, President; Mr Victor Riley Senior, Chairman; Mr A.E. Walter, Treasurer; and Edward H. Reeves, Hon. Secretary.'

More than 100 people gathered for the Club's first dinner/dance, held in February 1926, and it wasn't long before it could quite legitimately boast of being the largest one-make car club in the world.

This 12/4 Special, pictured at the Register's 'Coventry' Rally, is neatly finished. I wonder if the Riley family would have approved?

The Riley Register, however, came into existence much later. It was as recently as 1954 that a group of Riley enthusiasts — for 'real', as opposed to 'Nuffield' or 'BMC' Rileys — became convinced that the Riley Motor Club was no longer catering for them. With an eye to keeping pre-war Rileys not only alive, but well-and-truly kicking, they started the Register, which has been thriving ever since. This was the way in which interest was roused, in letters to the motoring press, in February 1954:

'May I trespass on the space of your correspondence columns to invite owners of pre-Nuffield Riley Nines to offer suggestions and help towards the forming of a Riley Nine Register?

'I am, of course, aware that there is a Riley Motor Club, but this is taken up, very largely, with other and more modern types of Riley.

'I had in mind a Register of the type so successfully run for many of the true vintage cars. Particularly the Register would try to organise some sort of spares directory, perhaps a supply of the commoner tuning parts, and collate information about the history, maintenance and tuning of these cars.

'These are just a few of the functions that occur to me, but with a car which has such a devoted band of followers there would be little limit to the functions which could be organised.

'Perhaps those interested would write to me.

Walsall, Staffordshire   C.F. Stanley.'

As you can see, the original idea was to protect the interests of Riley Nine owners, but every other type of vintage and thoroughbred Riley was soon covered.

The Riley Register and the Riley Motor Club naturally admit to the existence of each other, but rightly insist that they carry out rather different functions. In recent years, however, the Motor Club has altered its stance, and there is more of a functional overlap between the two.

(A third Riley organisation, incidentally, is the RM Club, which caters for the 'Nuffield' RM Models built between 1946 and 1955, and which does not therefore figure in this book.)

In my research I talked at length to John Hall of the Riley Motor Club, and to M.G. 'Griff' Griffiths of the Register. What follows is a summary of their remarks, and of the additional information they provided.

The Riley Motor Club Ltd celebrated its Diamond Jubilee of foundation in 1985, and carries on the traditions honed by the original club officers in the 1920s and 1930s. As the commemorative leaflet explains about the early days:

'The activities of the club in the form of Rallies, Treasure Hunts and success of Riley cars in open competitions, Trials and Races, were all considered to be news, and what better way of conveying this to members than through a monthly magazine called the *Riley Record*.

'The first edition consisted of only eight pages but this grew with the Club, until the final edition of that series in May 1950 consisted of some 24 pages.

'Subsequently news of the Club, Riley Cars and activities was conveyed through the pages of firstly *Motoring* and later *The Austin Magazine*. This continued until the late 1960s when Rileys finally ceased production, when the *Riley Record* was reinstated by the Club, and continues to be produced today.'

It was in those early days that a young man called Arnold Farrar, himself a Riley employee, became the Motor Club's secretary, and he held that position for no less than 45 years, retiring (to become a Vice President, specialising in Historical and Technical matters) in 1984. No other one-make club, I suggest, can match a continuous link like this.

Arnold Farrar saw the club grow, and grow, until by 1937 there were five UK centres. Expansion continued well into the 1950s, but as the technical interest and exclusivity of 'Riley' cars produced by BMC continued to decline, so too did interest in the club.

Name the model? Don't worry if it isn't familiar — this is a 12/4 Special, with the pre-selector gear change.

In 1984 John Hall, of Wolverhampton, became the Club's new secretary, and a year later he told me that there were about 1,000 members in the club, which had three UK centres — one based in London, one in the South-West, and one in the Midlands. The majority of the membership is based in the UK, with about 100 of them living overseas. There are separate, small, Riley clubs in other countries — in Australia, for instance, there was once a Riley Motor Club centre, which has now become a club in its own right.

For many years, of course, the Motor Club was very closely linked to the Riley factory (when the company was independent, and based in Coventry), and continued those links when Riley was controlled by Nuffield, and then BMC, with Arnold Farrar actually having an office at the Abingdon works.

As John Hall candidly admits:

'If we had not been so closely connected with the factory, and not so involved in the sale of new Rileys, there would really have been no need for the Register to start. At the time — in the 1950s — BMC were interested in selling more and more new Rileys, not necessarily supporting older ones. It wasn't always possible for the club to offer the type of services that people with old Rileys wanted.'

Not that it helped, in the long run. Following the foundation of British Leyland, in January 1968, the new management's interest in the old Riley marque declined to zero. No new models were introduced, and the last 'Rileys' of all were produced in the autumn of 1969. It was in that year that the Riley Motor Club (and the MG Car Club, incidentally) were invited to leave their Abingdon office, and take up an independent existence.

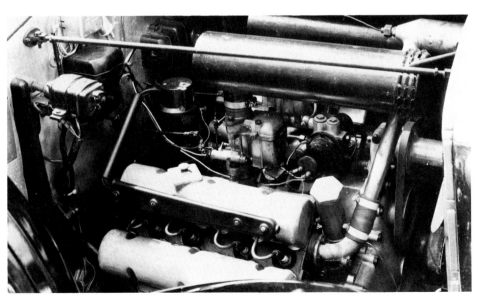

Would a Riley vee-8 powered sports car have been any more successful than the MPH? The engine was already available (this is the Autovia's Riley-based 2.85-litre example), but by that time the company had lost interest in fast two-seaters.

'The Riley Motor Club was then made into the Riley Motor Club Ltd. It was a continuation of the old, but was a new organisation. The directors, then, included Victor Riley Junior, Arnold Farrar, Bob Gerard, and John Brown.'

Today, the chairman of the club is still Victor Riley Junior, and a direct family link is accordingly retained. Mr Riley is Victor Riley Senior's son, but never had any connections with the Riley motor car business — he is, in fact, a farmer, although at one time he held a senior management position in the GKN group.

Links, however tenuous, have always been retained with British Leyland, and its successors — the Austin Rover Group being the most directly concerned group, which still retains the 'Riley' marque as one of its dormant trade marks — though there is no question of any financial support being granted. In a very arms-length relationship, the nearest the Motor Club gets to the 'old days' is if any obsolete paperwork is discovered, and passed over, rather than being thrown out for scrapping.

At the time of writing, the Motor Club was being re-organised — one might say 'streamlined' — from top to bottom, though secretary John Hall hoped that the members would approve. The club's activities were being re-aligned to take account of the realities of the 1980s; no new Rileys coming on to the scene, and no likelihood of new Rileys ever again.

Nothing sporting about this, you say? Correct, but consider the possibilities of the vee-8 engine which powered the vast Autovia car in the late 1930s.

Under the dignified skin of this Autovia limousine was a 2.85-litre vee-8 engine with the same type of valve gear and breathing arrangements as the sporting Rileys. The engine, in the right sort of car, had *great* possibilities.

'What I always try to get across is that we are more and more strongly in the spares supply business, and we shall continue to push that side of things strongly.

'At the National Classic Car Show, at the NEC, in 1984, a fellow came up to me, on our stand display, and said

"Riley Motor Club, selling spares?"

'— and I was able to tell him that we'd been selling spares for the last ten years. It was nice to see how surprised he was, but not as nice to hear him then say:

"I really honestly thought that you were just a social club."

The spares supply, and re-manufacturing side, is one which is helping Motor Club membership to grow once again. When Rileys went out of production, so too did those leaflets urging a new owner to 'Join the Riley Motor Club'. As new Riley owners sold their cars, and bought something else, so too did membership decline, so that by the early 1970s the club was at a low ebb. It was the 'classic car' boom of the mid and late 1970s which helped the turn around — helped along quite markedly by the new approach to spares and restoration advice.

To join the Riley Motor Club, you don't have to be a Riley owner, but only (in John Hall's words) 'a Riley enthusiast, and pay us £7.50 a year (£12.00 overseas). There is no joining fee, and family membership is also available for just £1 a year.'

What would you get for your £7.50? First and foremost, access to all the collected Riley wisdom that the Club, its officers, and its members, have around them, and this means not only that specific worries about restoration and parts supply can be solved, but that owners of similar models can be put in touch with each other to compare notes, and worries.

You also get six copies of the *Riley Record* every year (old issues, especially those dating from the 1920s and 1930s, are now valuable collectors' items — I was lucky enough to use a complete set in researching this book), regularly up-dated lists of new and secondhand spare parts for Rileys, and access to the Club's own Riley library, which is retained by Allan and Chris Draper, of the Midland Section.

That library, incidentally, not only includes road test reprints and catalogues, but wiring diagrams, workshop manuals, and other essential-to-know maintenance documents.

As to parts, as John Hall points out:

'A lot of people contact me, saying "I'm in dire trouble, I need a wotsit . . ." — and I'm usually able to say "Yes, I'm sure we can find some of those — or we have those — but you'll have to join the club first.'

New parts still turn up from time to time in dealer clear-outs — rarely for pre-war Rileys, of course, but don't forget that the Motor Club caters for Rileys of all ages — and where an old member dies his stocks are often recycled for the good of all. Items that are no longer available, but in demand, are re-manufactured, though once again the emphasis is on parts, including certain body panels, for post-war Rileys:

New Riley body panels may no longer be available from factory stocks, but they *are* still available if you know the right place to look . . .

'As far as the pre-war cars are concerned, we have no body parts at all, of course, though we can always put people in touch with someone who can make them. As far as mechanical parts are concerned, we have quite a few made.

Occasionally, too, the Club goes in for re-printing interesting material. As the club grows, and as the demand increases, more and more workshop manuals, or overhauling features from magazines, will be produced.

In the halcyon days of white tie occasions, and formal dinners, that of the Riley Motor Club used to be one of the best, and the most glittering, but those days have gone. Even to celebrate the 60th anniversary of the club's foundation, there was no demand for such a blow-out.

Every year, therefore, the Club's biggest occasion is National Riley Day and the Annual General Meeting — there is one for the national club, and each Centre tends to hold its own AGM some months in advance, as well. There is also at least one social rally every year, sometimes with a road run in the schedule, but not always. Most important is the gathering at a suitably pictureque spot, where a competition — most likely a Concours — will be held. In 1985 this was at Stanford Hall, near Rugby, the year before at Stoneleigh Abbey, and before that at Shugborough Hall, near Stafford.

The centres 'do their own thing' — in the Midlands, for instance, the big event of their year coincides with a Riley display at the Town and Country Festival at Stoneleigh. Throughout the network, of course, there are regular social runs, and it wouldn't be a British organisation if there was no scope for Noggin and Natter evenings. For details of times and places, members have only to consult the pages of *The Riley Record*.

To questions regarding the relationship, and co-operation, with the Register (which, whether anyone likes it or not, must be considered as a 'rival' organisation) I received a guarded response from John, but it seems that there may be closer and more amicable links in the future. In these

Riley club events (the Register being even more prominent than the Motor Club in this respect) usually feature Autojumble stands. Dig away — you will often be surprised by the choice of parts . . .

days, where tooling up for re-manufactured parts can be so expensive, this makes practical, and economical, sense.

For all further information and, perhaps, to become a member of the Riley Motor Club, contact:
John S. Hall, Secretary and Overseas Membership Secretary, 'Treelands', 127 Penn Road, Wolverhampton, West Midlands WV3 0DU.

The Riley Register may not be as old an organisation as the Motor Club, but it is equally active, if not more so. It may cost more to be a member, but there seem to be more detailed services available, and the membership list is even longer.

The Register specifically looks after pre-Nuffield Rileys, and anyone wanting to join to gain information about an RM-Series car, a 1.5, or whatever, will politely be shown up the road to the Motor Club. Club officials make it quite clear that, in their opinion, no-one owning a pre-war Riley can possibly get along without being a member. They may be right — the statistics suggest that most Riley owners agree with them.

. . . even if you may have to identify detail parts for yourself!

At the last count there were between 1,200 and 1,300 Register members and the cost is £10 a year. Qualification, by comparison with the Motor Club, is more strict, for Full Membership is only offered to someone who has 'at least' one suitable Riley model. Associate Membership, however, is also available at the same price, if you merely have an interest, but no actual Riley — and according to Mr Griffiths, there is 'little difference' in benefits. Family members only have to pay 25 pence a year, and Old Age Pensioners get Full Membership for a mere £2 a year.

Incidentally, if the 'movement' of Register membership is quite limited, these days, this is almost certainly because the movement of vintage and thoroughbred Rileys is also quite gentle. Those lucky people who have already captured their Riley are usually reluctant to sell it!

As with any large one-make club, membership also splits itself into areas, but the heart and soul of the Register is its splendid quarterly magazine, which carries the grand title of the *Bulletin of the Riley Register*. Now, as for more than fifteen years, the 'Riley' part of that title is the famous diamond trademark, and the millenium will come before the cover is printed in other than Riley blue! With 120 issues published by the end of 1985, this is a very important part of the club itself. A.P. 'Tony' Bird was not only the Register's President until 1985, but has been the *Bulletin's* Editor for more than twenty years, and in many ways the Register revolves round him, and his publication. Incidentally, he is also a vice president of the Riley Motor Club.

As with the Motor Club, there are British and overseas areas, notably in Australia and New Zealand — the Australian organisation calling itself the Riley Motor Club of Australia.

The Register's main philosophy at the start, and today, is 'to keep Rileys on the road', and every development has been made with that in mind. At first, in the 1950s, the Register was able to supply parts and

In many cases, it is necessary to start by buying a secondhand part — even electrical items like this can properly be restored for sporting Riley models.

advice, but in the second phase more complex parts were re-manufactured, and in the 1980s that process is being taken steadily further.

For many years the Register had 'friends in high places'. At a time when first BMC, then British Leyland, were ruthlessly destroying Riley's heritage, converting and abandoning its factories, and throwing out every scrap of written information and hardware which was no longer of any interest to them, the Register was fortunate in knowing people still 'on the inside' who could divert things in their direction.

A 1960s *Bulletin,* for instance, featured Eddie Maher as its president, and Arnold Farrar as a vice-president. Not only did Farrar work as the Riley Motor Club secretary, from an office at the BMC (MG) Abingdon factory, but Eddie Maher was a senior BMC engineer at the Morris Engines Branch in Coventry, and had been a development engineer with Riley in the 1920s and 1930s.

This means that, one way or another (and perhaps it does not do to enquire too closely as to the methods once employed — though Austin Rover are very relaxed about it all these days) every worthwhile mechanical drawing of a 'real' Riley component has found its way into the hands of the Register, which means that restoration, and the checking of cars for authenticity, is always possible (if not cheap). Arnold Farrar also has stocks of these for the use of the Riley Motor Club.

As has already been made clear in the section on restoration, not only are body parts not available for restoration purposes, but neither are the drawings. There are, of course, surviving examples of all true sporting Rileys (except Grebes!) to make restoration a matter of copying, rather than inventing. The Register, at least, can and do put members with problems in touch either with the experts on various models, or with members having such models of their own.

The big event of the Register's year, without a doubt, is the Coventry Rally. This has always been held in June or July, and for many years involved a visit to the historic Riley factory in Coventry, merely to allow a member to say afterwards that he had been back to 'the birthplace'.

In recent years a Coventry hotel has hosted the Rally, with the actual gathering of all the cars at the picturesque Coombe Abbey, not far from the city, where there is a navigational run on the Saturday, a series of driving tests on the Sunday morning, and a Concours on the Sunday afternoon, along with the opportunity to buy and sell spares, swop stories, or merely ogle another example of the marque.

Rileys of this type, of course, still perform actively in historic motor sport, and this is backed up by the pictures published in these pages of important cars being raced at Cadwell Park, or used in hillclimbs at Prescott.

Every year, as with the Motor Club, there is the all-important Annual General Meeting, whose venue moves around the country. As chairman 'Griff' Griffiths told me: 'The attendance varies markedly though we have a faithful core — we only got about twenty to Durham one year, but there were 100 members at Nottingham, and probably a differently made-up 100 at Taunton.'

Because every full member actually has a Coventry-Riley of his own (and because experience shows that most of them are very vocal in their opinions), the Register always seems to know what technical and re-manufacturing assistance is needed. Lists are gradually being compiled of those suppliers who can provide difficult-to-find parts, and a start is being made on the re-manufacture of complex parts. Rear axle parts are already available, as are six-cylinder block castings from Barrie Gillies, and if ever the supply of four-cylinder head castings run out (no problem at this stage) the club is even prepared to consider having these made. The drawings, as I have said, are available.

Not only does the Register produce a quarterly *Bulletin,* but there are also eight Newsletters every year — which means that a member hears from the Register at least once every six weeks. The Register is justly proud, too, of its achievement in reprinting a variety of hard-to-find Riley booklets for members to buy. It is one thing to find an original Riley Nine Spare Parts Catalogue at an autojumble, but that hardly compensates for five

One of many Riley 'specials' to be seen in the Register these days — this one having a 'Big Four' $2\frac{1}{2}$-litre engine.

years of waiting! Even so, strong men have been known to blanch when they see the original prices for an expensive 1980s spare part.

The Spares and Accessory price list is impressive, getting larger all the time, and is regularly updated. A quick flick through its pages shows how deeply the Register has gone into the question of parts supply — the only excuse an owner can have for failure to complete mechanical restoration is lack of time, or lack of money.

By any standards, any club whose list of officers fills the back page of a *Bulletin* has to be well-established, and well-organised. As with the Motor Club, you can't hope to gain access to parts unless you are a Register member, but you can at least gain information, and a warm welcome to join the Register itself.

The President of the Register is: R. Cresswell, 51 Grange Hill, Coggeshall, Colchester, Essex.

The *Bulletin* Editor is: A.P. Bird, 4 Sunnyside, Kingsclere, Nr Newbury, Berks RG15 8PW.

The Membership Secretary is: J.A. Clarke, 56 Cheltenham Road, Bishops Cleeve, Cheltenham, Gloucestershire GL52 4LY.

A measure of the 'depth' of the Register is that there are no fewer than nine Spares Officers, each with his own special expertise — and the true fanatical experts for some models do not even appear!

No-one should even think of owning, let alone restoring and running, a Coventry Riley without joining one or other of the specialist clubs. In the end, it could save you a lot of money.

XII
Healey: The Sporting Riley Revived

The fastest sports cars ever to use Riley engines were not Rileys at all —
but Healeys. Nor were these cars built while the true 'Coventry Riley' was
still in existence. The Healey motor car, built from 1946 to 1954, did
marvellous things for the Riley marque's image, though years too late to
help it survive as an independent concern.

As already mentioned, the Healey link was established in the early
1930s. Donald Healey, having already won the Monte Carlo rally in an
Invicta, then began to rally in Rileys, and finally moved to the Midlands, to
work for Riley as a design/development engineer. It was while Healey was
working for the company that cars like the MPH and the Imp were
conceived.

Donald Healey then moved on, to Triumph, also of Coventry, in the
autumn of 1933, and his most famous product for that firm was the
supercharged eight-cylinder Dolomite. Perhaps, therefore, the styling
similarities between that Dolomite, and the Imp/MPH/Sprite models, are
now easier to understand. Apart from a brief move to Lucas, Donald
Healey stayed at Triumph, latterly as technical director, until the company
slid into bankruptcy in 1939. After staying on for a while, at the outset of
the Second World War, under the new owners, Thos. Ward Ltd, he moved
yet again, to join the Rootes Group (also in Coventry, and still colloquially
known as 'The Humber'), where he was involved in military vehicle design
work.

In theory there was no time for work on private cars to take place, but
the resourceful Healey certainly found enough of it to start planning to
build new models after the war was over. At first, though, he still looked on
these new cars as 'Triumphs', and was hoping to interest Thos. Ward in
backing him.

It was a good idea, but it did not work, for Thos. Ward really had no
interest in reviving the Triumph business after the German airforce had
flattened some of the factory buildings in the bomber raids of World War
Two.

As Donald's equally well known son, Geoff, has written: 'He was determined to have somewhere near 100 bhp per ton of vehicle weight as he considered this essential to give the performance he wanted. He planned the design with two of his colleagues at Humber — A. C. (Sammy) Sampietro, a brilliant automobile engineer, and Ben Bowden, an extremely talented body engineer and stylist.'

At the same time he formed his own company, and although there were several defunct marque names he would have liked to use, in the end he chose his own name for the marque title. Thus the Healey motor company was born. Sampietro designed the 8 foot 6-inch chassis, which had coil spring and trailing link independent front suspension, while Bowden began the styling, and the layout of the first body shells. As one of Healey's associates, James Watt, once said, Ben sketched away at his body drawings '. . . in the dining room of his home in Coventry, drawing directly on to the wallpaper, and then taking tracings from the originals!'

It was, of course, quite out of the question for the tiny Healey company to design its own engines and transmissions. Once Triumph had declined to back the project, Donald Healey had to look around for alternative supplies, but fortunately he could turn to his old friends at Riley for assistance.

The first approach was to Victor Leverett, a one-time Triumph colleague of Healey, and by this time on the staff of Riley. This led to talks with Victor Riley, who eventually agreed to supply Riley engines, gearboxes, and any other Riley components which might be needed.

These meetings took place in 1945, when Riley's post-war production

The post-Hitler War RM Series Rileys used $1\frac{1}{2}$-litre or 'Big Four' $2\frac{1}{2}$-litre engines. The Healey used the $2\frac{1}{2}$-litre version in slightly modified form.

and development policy was already becoming clear. There was to be a new design of Riley passenger car (now universally remembered as the 'RM' series) — which happily had virtually no influence from Nuffield — and it was to be offered either with the well-known $1\frac{1}{2}$-litre, or the 'Big Four' $2\frac{1}{2}$-litre, twin high camshaft four-cylinder engines.

Donald Healey did not consider the $1\frac{1}{2}$-litre engine to be powerful enough for his needs. (In 'Sprite' tune Riley had claimed 60 bhp in the late 1930s, and for the $1\frac{1}{2}$-litre RMA saloon Nuffield claimed a mere 55 bhp in 1946.) The 'Big Four', however, was a much more promising unit.

When newly-announced, in 1937, there was no sporting application for the 2,443-cc 'Big Four' engine, and initially it produced 80 bhp. There was only a single downdraught Zenith carburettor, and the inlet and exhaust manifolds were both on the same side of the cylinder head, with the inlet ports running through the head in a rather convoluted manner; this was in order to provide a 'hot spot' on the exhaust manifold.

This was not at all a promising layout, as far as high output and good breathing was concerned; indeed, by comparison with the original Riley Nine, and the six-cylinder engines, it was not nearly as efficient, or technically 'elegant'.

Even before the Nuffield takeover of 1938 was announced, the designers had made major changes, which quite transformed the engine — not only in its performance, but in its looks (and for any true sporting car, even the styling of the engine is an important sales factor).

There was a new cylinder head, to which efficient cross-flow breathing had been restored. As with any 'proper' twin high camshaft Riley engine, there were exhaust ports on one side of the cylinder head (the near side), and in this case there were siamesed ports on the opposite side of the casting. For the 1939 model 16-hp 'Nuffield' Riley, the first to use the revised unit, there was a single downdraught SU carburettor, but for the post-war RM-Series engine, twin-horizontal SU H4 carburettors were fitted.

The result was an engine which looked impressive, and which was also much more suited to the job it had to do. For Riley's own cars, it was a very successful engine for the $2\frac{1}{2}$-litre RM models built until 1953, and the BMC-designed Riley Pathfinder which followed it; the last $2\frac{1}{2}$-litre unit of all was produced in 1957, after which all succeeding Rileys had BMC engines of no technical or architectural merit!

As with most quoted figures for this point in motoring history, it is best to treat the published power outputs with caution. Riley themselves quoted 90 bhp at 4,300 rpm, while Healey, helped along only by changes to the carburettor air cleaner, and to the exhaust system, claimed no less than 100 bhp at 4,600 rpm; both engines then had a compression ratio of 6.5:1. However, by 1948, when the first post-war Earls Court Motor Show was held, the compression ratio had risen to 6.9:1, Riley were claiming 100 bhp at 4,500 rpm, and Healey were quoting 104 bhp at the same revs!

Perhaps all this is a touch confusing, but there was no doubt at all that — to borrow a phrase from Rolls-Royce — it was 'sufficient', for each and every Riley-powered Healey was capable of more than 100 mph.

Behind the engine the rest of the transmission was almost pure $2\frac{1}{2}$-litre Riley, which is to say that there was a four-speed gearbox with synchromesh on top, third and second gears, and torque tube transmission to the spiral bevel back axle. In the Healey application, where the wheelbase was 17 inches less than that of the Riley $2\frac{1}{2}$-litre saloon, there was virtually no space for a primary propeller shaft behind the gearbox, and back-to-back universal joints were used instead.

The original Healey production cars were the Westland Roadster, and the Elliot saloon, both made on the same Riley-powered chassis, and both in production from October 1946, when Riley could finally supply the engines and transmissions in sufficient numbers. From then, until 1954, there were many differently-bodied Healeys based on the same running gear — known as the Westland tourer, Elliot saloon, Duncan saloon, Sportsmobile roadster, Silverstone sports car, Tickford saloon, and Abbott drop-head coupé. In most cases the names were inspired by the company producing the body shell for Healey, who had no facilities for building their own coachwork.

In no time at all, it seemed, Donald Healey was well on the way to establishing yet another career. He had already proved his point in competition, then as a technical chief, in the 1920s and 1930s; now he was becoming a fully-fledged manufacturer.

The cars sold well, especially in export markets, and Healey certainly

The Riley-engined Healey Elliot saloon at speed — it could exceed 100 mph.

One of the many Riley-engined Healey derivatives was the two-door 'Tickford' saloon.

turned out as many cars as their little factory at The Cape, Warwick, would accommodate. The cynics would no doubt say that *any* immediate post-war car could be sold as there was such a voracious demand for anything on wheels, but the truth was that the Healey was a fast, good-handling, and distinctive machine, with a real character of its own.

Even the first Elliot was timed at 104 mph, which made it one of the fastest British cars of its day (the Riley 2^1/$_2$-litre roadster, for instance, was good for no more than 98 mph), and it was not long before the Healey company began to enter their cars in international races and rallies. The very first entry was of a Westland in the 1947 Alpine rally, where Donald Healey and Tommy Wisdom won the 3-litre category; to add insult to injury, against its competitors, the car was then cleaned up, entered for the Concours 'beauty contest' — and won the category for open cars!

To follow this, there were sterling performances in 1948, in the Targa Florio (where Count Johnny Lurani was second overall in the touring car category, in an Elliot), and ninth place overall in the Mille Miglia for Donald and Geoffrey Healey in a Westland. Then there was a class win (Elliot) in the Spa 24 Hour race, a class win in the Alpine rally (Westland) and . . . need I go on?

The most exciting of all the Riley-engined Healeys, however, was the starkly-styled Silverstone, which made its bow in 1949. While it retained the same chassis as the earlier models, the Silverstone was a pure two-seater sports car, with a slim 'almost two-seater' body style, and cycle-type front wings. The headlamps were concealed behind the front grille, and although there were no bumpers of any sort, the horizontally-mounted spare wheel and tyre, poking out of the tail, acted as a very effective fender at the back of the car!

For the Silverstone, the engine/gearbox assembly was moved back no less than eight inches in the chassis frame, which meant that further changes to the Riley-based torque-tube transmission were required, but it was still recognisably the same design of car, and still owed a lot to Riley. The Silverstone was about 450 lb lighter than other Healeys, which meant that it had even more performance.

This, however, was really the high-point for Riley-powered Healeys, for the first of the Nash-powered Healeys came along in 1950, and for the next few years Nash-Healey production dominated the scene at Warwick. Then, in 1952, Healey produced their Austin A90-powered '100' prototype BMC's Len Lord adopted it as the Austin-Healey 100 sports car and the rest, as they say, is history . . .

In any case, the Riley 2½-litre engine had reached the limit of its development potential, even before BMC (the amalgam of the Nuffield Organisation with Austin) had lost interest in it. For the Pathfinder of 1953, there were numerous minor changes to aid the installation, and the compression ratio had been raised only slightly, to 7.25:1, but peak power rose only to 102 bhp at 4,400 rpm. Rather mysteriously, the quoted figure had risen to 110 bhp by the end of 1954, though no obvious changes had been made in the meantime!

The most accelerative of all Riley-engined Healeys was the Silverstone two-seater sports car.

XIII
Specifications of Sporting Rileys

Apart from the side-valve Redwingers, a skein of consistent design layouts, and interchangeable parts, runs through this series of Sporting Rileys, as the facts and figures summarised below ofen confirm.

I ought to state, as I have sometimes stated in the earlier text, that special features certainly could be, and often were, built into individual examples of these Rileys. It is quite possible that machines which survive do not exactly (not nearly, sometimes) match the specification which the publicity material originally said they *should* have had!

To quote an authority on Rileys, many years ago:

'When dealing with Rileys it is very difficult to be positive, as there seems to be an exception to every rule, and it is only by suggestion and counter-suggestion that something like the truth can be established.'

In the intervening years, too, it is also likely that the owners of some cars have made further changes, either because of a personal whim, or merely to keep the car on the road.

If I have omitted a model which the reader thinks is a sporting Riley, I apologise. I think it is almost inevitable, for Rileys, and Riley owners, are like that!

Redwinger models: produced 1923 to 1928

General layout: Front engine, and separate gearbox, rear drive, in separate chassis frame, with coachbuilt two-seater or four-seater open body styles. Design evolved from side-valve touring cars first announced in 1919.

Engine: 4-cylinders, in line, with side-mounted inlet and exhaust valves, operated directly from side-mounted camshaft. Bore and stroke 65.8 x 110 mm, 1,498 cc (2.59 x 4.33 in., 91.5 cu in.). Single Solex carburettor. Peak power, 40 bhp at 3,600 rpm.

Transmission: Dry cone clutch, in unit with engine, and separately mounted four-speed manual transmission. Open propeller shaft drive to spiral bevel final drive, and 'live' rear axle. Central gear change, direct acting (some cars with remote, right-hand change). Final drive ratios – 4.0:1, 4.3:1 and 4.7:1 all fitted. Typical overall ratios for four-seater with 4.7:1 ratio were: 4.7, 7.4, 11.6, 18.2, reverse 18.2:1. No synchromesh on any gear.

Suspension and brakes: Beam front axle, half-elliptic leaf springs, and friction-type lever-arm dampers. Live rear axle, half-elliptic leaf springs, and friction-type lever arm dampers. Worm and wheel steering.

Drum rear brakes. Optional drum front brakes from 1924 onward: actuation by rods and levers. Rod operated handbrake.

27 x 4.40 in. front and rear tyres, on 27-in wire-spoke wheels, with four-stud fixings.

Dimensions: Wheelbase 9 ft. 0 in. (274.3 cm); front track 4ft. 4 in. (132.1 cm); rear track 4 ft. 4 in. (132.1 cm).

Fuel tank capacity 7.0 Imperial gallons (31.8 litres).

Prices: 1923   – two-seater £495
             1924   – two-seater £495
                         – four-seater £495
             1925   – two-seater £495
                         – four-seater £495
                – these prices retained for 1926 and 1927, then:
             1928   – two-seater £395
                         – four-seater £398

Short Wheelbase Sports: produced 1924 and 1925 only

Basic mechanical specification as for two-seater Redwinger, except for:

Final drive ratio 4.4:1. Overall ratios 4.4, 6.9, 10.8, 15.5, reverse 15.5:1. 700 x 80 mm tyres. Wheelbase 8 ft. 0 in. (243.8 cm). Fuel tank capacity 5.5 Imperial gallons (25 litres).

Price: £545.

Supercharged 11/50/65 Sports Model: produced 1926 only

This was a one-off prototype, based on the four-seater Redwinger structure, with an overhead-valve conversion of the 1,498 cc engine, fitted with a Roots-type supercharger, and a 4.7:1 final drive ratio. Only one was built; the car never went into production.

9 hp Brooklands Speed Model: produced 1927 to 1932

General layout: Front engine and transmission, rear drive, in separate chassis frame, with coachbuilt two-seater body shell. Evolved from Riley Nine family car, first revealed in October 1926. Brooklands prototype first shown August 1927.

Engine: 4-cylinders, in line, with inlet and exhaust valves overhead, and opposed at 90 degrees, operated by push rods and rockers from twin high camshafts. Bore and stroke 60.3 x 95.2 mm, 1,087 cc (2.375 x 3.75., 66.36 cu. in.). Twin Solex or SU horizontal carburettors. Peak power, up to 50 bhp (gross) at 5,000 rpm.

Transmission: Single dry plate clutch, and four-speed manual transmission, all in unit with the engine. Torque tube transmission to spiral bevel final drive, and 'live' rear axle. Right hand change on prototypes; central, remote control change on all other cars. Final drive ratio 4.77:1. Overall gear ratios 4.77, 5.96, 7.155, 11.78, reverse 18.50:1. No synchromesh on any gear.

Suspension and brakes: Beam front axle, half-elliptic leaf springs, and friction type lever-arm dampers. Live rear axle, half-elliptic leaf springs, torque tube location, and friction type lever-arm dampers. Worm type steering.

Drum front and rear brakes, 10.125 in. diameter on earlier cars, later 13 in. diameter drums. Actuation by cables and rods. Rod operated handbrake. 27 x 4.40 in (4.50 x 19 in.) front and rear tyres, on 19 in. wheels with 3.00 in. rims, with five-stud or (later) six-stud wire-spoke construction.

Dimensions: Wheelbase 8 ft. 0 in. (243.8 cm); front track 3 ft. 11.75 in (121.3 cm); rear track 3 ft. 11.75 in. (121.3 cm). Fuel tank capacity 10 Imperial gallons (45.4 litres).

Prices:
1928 model	£395
1929 Brooklands Speed model	£420
1930 to 1932 Brooklands Speed Model	£420
Brooklands Speed Model Plus	£475

Brooklands Six: produced 1932 only

General layout: Front engine and transmission, rear drive, in separate chassis frame, with lightweight two-seater body shell. Engine developed from the Six unit first revealed in September 1928.

Engine: 6-cylinders, in line, with inlet and exhaust valves overhead, and opposed at 90 degrees, operated by push rods and rockers from twin high camshafts. Bore and stroke 57.5 x 95.2 mm, 1,486 cc (2.263 x 3.75 in., 90.72 cu. in.). Three SU horizontal carburettors.

Transmission: Single dry plate clutch, and four-speed manual transmission, all in unit with the engine. Torque tube transmission to spiral bevel final drive, and 'live' rear axle. Central, remote control, gear change. Final drive ratio 4.77:1. Overall gear ratios 4.77, 5.96, 7.166, 11.78, reverse 18.50:1. No synchromesh on any gear.

Suspension and brakes: Beam front axle, half-elliptic leaf springs, and Duplex Andre lever arm dampers. Live rear axle, half-elliptic leaf springs, torque tube location, and Duplex Andre lever arm dampers. Worm type steering.
    Drum front and rear brakes, 13 in. diameter drums. Actuation by cables and rods. Rod operated handbrake.
    5.00 x 19 in. tyres, front and rear, on 19 in. wheels with 3.50 in. rims. Six-stud wire-spoke wheels.

Dimensions: Wheelbase 9 ft. 0 in. (274.3 cm); front track 3 ft. 11.75 in. (121.3 cm); rear track 3 ft. 11.75 in. (121.3 cm).
    Fuel tank capacity 26.5 Imperial gallons (120.0 litres).

Price: £595   1932 only

Grebe Six: produced 1933 only

General layout: Front engine and transmission, rear drive, in separate chassis frame, with lightweight two-seater body shell. Engine further developed from Brooklands Six unit.

Engine: 6-cylinders, in line, with inlet and exhaust valves overhead, and opposed at 90 degrees, operated by push rods and rockers from twin high camshafts. Bore and stroke 57.5 x 95.2mm, 1,486cc (2.263 x 9.75 in., 90.72 cu.in.). Three SU horizontal carburettors.

Transmission: Single dry plate clutch and four-speed manual transmission, all in unit with the engine. Torque tube transmission to spiral bevel final drive, and 'live' rear axle. Central, remote control, gear change. Final drive ratio 4.77:1. Overall gear ratios 4.77, 5.96, 7.155, 11.78, reverse 18.50:1. No synchromesh on any gear.

Suspension and brakes: Beam front axle, half-elliptic leaf springs, friction-type lever-arm dampers. Live rear axle, half-elliptic leaf springs, torque tube location, and friction-type lever-arm dampers. Worm type steering.

Drum front and rear brakes, 15 in. diameter drums. Actuation by cables and rods. Rod operated handbrake.

5.00 x 19 in. tyres, front and rear, on 19 in. wheels with 3.00 in. rims. Centre-lock wire-spoke wheels.

Dimensions: Wheelbase 8 ft. 6 in. (259.1 cm); front track 3 ft. 11.75 in. (121.3 cm); rear track 3 ft. 11.75 in. (121.3 cm).

Fuel tank capacity (total) 27 Imperial gallons (122.5 litres)

Price: £595   1933 only

9 hp Imp: produced 1934 to 1935

General layout: Front engine and transmission, rear drive, in separate chassis frame, with two-seater sports body shell. Engine evolved from that of the Riley Nine family car, and indirectly from the 9 hp Brooklands model.

Engine: 4-cylinders, in line, with inlet and exhaust valves overhead, and opposed at 90 degrees, operated by push rods and rockers from twin high camshafts. Bore and stroke 60.3 x 95.2 mm, 1,087 cc (2.375 x 3.75 in., 66.36 cu. in.). Twin horizontal SU carburettors.

Transmission: Choice of manual, or pre-selector gearboxes, both mounted in unit with the engine. Torque tube transmission to spiral bevel final drive, and 'live' rear axle. Final drive ratio 5.25:1 in each case.

Manual: Single dry plate clutch, four-speed manual gearbox, with central, remote control, gear change. Overall gear ratios 5.25, 7.67, 13.13, 20.37, reverse 20.32:1. No synchromesh on any gear. Pre-selector: Centrifugal clutch, and four-speed ENV transmission, with selector lever mounted on the steering column. Overall gear ratios 5.25, 7.67, 12.66, 20.47, reverse 20.47:1.

Suspension and brakes: Beam front axle, half-elliptic leaf springs, friction-type lever-arm dampers. Live rear axle, half-elliptic leaf springs, torque tube location, and friction-type lever-arm dampers. Worm-type steering.

Drum front and rear brakes, 13 in. diameter drums. Actuation by cables and rods. Rod operated handbrake.

4.50 x 19 in. tyres, front and rear, on 19 in. wheels with 2.5 in. rims. Centre-lock wire-spoke wheels.

Dimensions: Wheelbase 7 ft. 6 in. (228.6 cm); front track 3 ft. 11.75 in. (121.3 cm); rear track 3 ft. 11.75 in (121.3 cm). Overall length 11 ft. 2 in. (340.4 cm); overall width 4 ft. 9.5 in. (146 cm). Unladen weight (approx) 1,800 lb. (816 kg). Fuel tank capacity 12 Imperial gallons (54.5 litres)

Price: £298 with manual transmission
              £325 with preselector transmission

MPH: produced 1934 and 1935

General layout: Front engine and transmission, rear drive, in separate channel and part box-section chassis frame, with two-seater sports body shell. Engine evolved from that of the Brooklands and Grebe 'six', and closely related to all other Riley six-cylinder engines.

Engine: 6-cylinders, in line, with inlet and exhaust valves overhead, and opposed at 90-degrees, operated by push rods and rockers from twin high camshafts. Choice of three engine sizes, all in same closely-linked family:

Bore and stroke 57 x 95.2 mm, 1,458 cc (2.244 x 3.75 in., 89.0 cu. in.)
Bore and stroke 60.3 x 95.2 mm, 1,633 cc (2.375 x 3.75 in., 99.54 cu. in.).
Bore and stroke 62 x 95.2 mm, 1,726 cc (2.44 x 3.75 in., 105.36 cu. in.)
– all with twin horizontal SU carburettors (though three SU carburettor equipment was also available). Peak power 'over 70 bhp' according to original analyses.

Transmission: Choice of manual, or pre-selector gearboxes, both mounted in unit with the engine. Torque tube transmission to spiral bevel final drive, and 'live' rear axle. Final drive ratio 4.77:1 with manual gearbox, 5.0:1 with pre-selector transmission.

Manual: Single dry plate clutch, four-speed manual gearbox, with central remote control, gear change. Overall gear ratios 4.77, 5.95, 7.15, 11.78, reverse 18.51:1. No synchromesh on any gear.

Pre-selector: Centrifugal clutch, and four-speed Armstrong-Siddeley transmission, with selector lever mounted on the steering column. Overall gear ratios 5.0, 6.25, 7.5, 13.35, reverse 22.99:1.

Suspension and brakes: Beam front axle, half-elliptic leaf springs, torque rods, friction-type lever-arm dampers. Live rear axle, half-elliptic leaf springs, torque tube location, and friction-type lever-arm dampers. Worm-type steering.

Drum front and rear brakes, 15 in. diameter drums. Actuation by cables and rods. Rod operated handbrake.

5.00 x 19 in. tyres, front and rear, on 19 in. wheels with 3.00 in. rims. Alternatively, 4.75 x 18 in. tyres, on 3.0 in. rims. Both with centre-lock wire spoke wheels.

Dimensions: Wheelbase 8 ft. 1.5 in. (247.65 cm); front track 3 ft. 11.75 in. (121.3 cm); rear track 3 ft. 11.75 in. (121.3 cm). Overall length 12 ft. 0 in. (365.76 cm); overall width 4 ft. 9.5 in (146 cm). Unladen weight (approx) 2,020 lb (916 kg). Fuel capacity 15 Imperial gallons (68.1 litres).

Price: £550

Sprite: produced 1935 to 1938

General layout: Front engine and transmission, rear drive, in separate channel and part box-section chassis frame, with two-seater sports body shell having choice of nose styles. Engine based on that of the new 1½-litre unit, first seen in September 1934, but chassis and style close to that of the discontinued MPH.

Engine: 4-cylinders, in line, with inlet and exhaust valves overhead, and opposed at 90 degrees, operated by pushrods and rockers from twin high camshafts. Bore and stroke 69 mm x 100 mm, 1,496 cc (2.716 x 3.937 in., 91.33 cu. in.). Twin horizontal SU carburettors. 60 bhp at 5,000 rpm.

Transmission: Choice of manual, or pre-selector gearboxes, both mounted in unit with the engine. Torque tube transmission to spiral bevel final drive, and 'live' rear axle. Final drive ratio 5.22:1.

Manual: Single dry plate clutch, four-speed manual gearbox, with central, remote-control, gear change. Overall gear ratios 5.22, 7.63, 13.05, 20.25, reverse 20.25:1. No synchromesh on any gear.

Pre-selector: Centrifugal clutch, and four-speed Wilson-type Armstrong Siddeley transmission, with selector lever mounted on the steering column. Overall gear ratios 5.22, 7.40, 10.30, 17.53, reverse 26.0:1.

Suspension and brakes: Beam front axle, half-elliptic leaf springs, friction-type lever-arm dampers. Live rear axle, half-elliptic leaf springs, torque tube location, and friction type lever-arm dampers. Worm-type steering.

Drum front and rear brakes, 13 in. diameter drums. Actuation by rods. Rod operated handbrake.

5.0 x 19 in. tyres, front and rear, on 19 in. centre-lock wire spoke wheels, with 3.00 in. rims.

Dimensions: Wheelbase 8 ft. 1.25 in (247.65 cm); front track 3 ft. 11.75 in. (121.3 cm); rear track 3 ft. 11.75 in. (121.3 cm). Overall length 12 ft. 0 in (365.76 cm); overall width 4 ft. 9.5 in. (146 cm). Unladen weight (approx) 2,210 lb (1,002 kg). Fuel capacity 15 Imperial gallons (68.1 litres).

Price: £425 in 1936 and 1937
            £450 for 1938

Index